"She learned that pain and suffering are an inevitable part of evolving and self-growth. *The Sea Glass Soul's* parallel of the self and the evolution of glass gives a unique and tranquil twist on how we should view our own struggles and heartaches. Closely woven together with her own struggles and her own spirituality, Jamie encourages the reader to look inward and review their own self. With each chapter, she helps the reader through a journaling journey of self-realization and clarity."

—**Alicia Dominy,** Licensed Master Social Worker

"*The Sea Glass Soul* gently encourages you to take the journey into the places in your life that need the space to heal. From a place of experience, Jamie shares her exploration of allowing God to walk her through the sometimes jagged paths of life while leaning on her faith as she traveled. It takes such courage to share your story in such a vulnerable way, yet Jamie has done so in a powerful way to encourage others on their journeys of healing."

—**Meredith Drake,** Pastor, Dayspring Church

"When the vessel breaks like we think it shouldn't, perhaps it's not its undoing. Rather, it's the beginning of a new thing. Jamie's open-hearted sharing of her journey to healing is very touching and encouraging. I hardily recommend her book to all who are searching for a way to do life better."

—**Sherry Oxendine,** Missionary, Go To Nations

"Zenteno bares her soul, as she shares her journey of redemption and healing, offering encouragement and hope for a better tomorrow for those who are held captive by the hurts and disappointments of the past."

—**Tim Gregory,** Pastor/Author,
Family Worship Center

The Sea Glass Soul

FORGED BY FIRE, TEMPERED BY THE SEA

JAMIE ZENTENO

LUCIDBOOKS

The Sea Glass Soul
Forged by Fire, Tempered by the Sea
Copyright © 2024 by Jamie Zenteno

Published by Lucid Books in Houston, TX
www.LucidBooks.com

All rights reserved. No part of this publication may be reproduced, stored in a retrieval system, or transmitted in any form by any means, electronic, mechanical, photocopy, recording, or otherwise, without the prior permission of the publisher, except as provided for by USA copyright law.

Unless otherwise indicated, scripture quotations are taken from the NIV (Holy Bible, New International Version®,) NIV®. Copyright ©1973, 1978, 1984, 2011 by Biblica, Inc.™ Used by permission of Zondervan. All rights reserved worldwide. www.zondervan.com The "NIV" and "New International Version" are trademarks registered in the United States Patent and Trademark Office by Biblica, Inc.™

Scripture quotations marked (ESV) are taken from the ESV® Bible (The Holy Bible, English Standard Version®), copyright © 2001 by Crossway, a publishing ministry of Good News Publishers. Used by permission. All rights reserved.

Scripture quotations marked (KJV) are taken from the King James Version (KJV): King James Version, public domain.

Scripture quotations marked (MSG) are taken from THE MESSAGE, copyright © 1993, 2002, 2018 by Eugene H. Peterson. Used by permission of NavPress. All rights reserved. Represented by Tyndale House Publishers, Inc.

Scripture quotations marked (NLT) are taken from the Holy Bible, New Living Translation, copyright ©1996, 2004, 2015 by Tyndale House Foundation. Used by permission of Tyndale House Publishers, Carol Stream, Illinois 60188. All rights reserved.

Scripture quotations marked (NLV) are taken from the New Life Version, Copyright © 1969 and 2003. Used by permission of Barbour Publishing, Inc., Uhrichsville, Ohio 44683. All rights reserved.

ISBN: 978-1-63296-734-3 (Hardback)
ISBN: 978-1-63296-733-6 (Paperback)
eISBN: 978-1-63296-735-0

Special Sales: Most Lucid Books titles are available in special quantity discounts. Custom imprinting or excerpting can also be done to fit special needs. Contact Lucid Books at Info@LucidBooks.com

To my two beautiful girls, Shelby and Sydney, who have inspired their mama to persevere through all the storms no matter how heavy the raindrops may have been.

Special Thanks

I am forever grateful for the wonderful people in my life who encouraged, supported, and prayed for me throughout my healing journey while I penned this book. Your words, hugs, and heartfelt compassionate friendship warm my heart like an ocean sunset on a summer evening. Thank you for believing in me this side of Heaven like the Lord does.

Table of Contents

Introduction	1
Chapter 1: Forged by Fire	5
Chapter 2: Carafes	19
Chapter 3: Broken Pieces and Sharp Edges	31
Chapter 4: The Sea	47
Chapter 5: Salt	59
Chapter 6: Surfaces	71
Chapter 7: Tumbling About	85
Chapter 8: The Rocks	99
Chapter 9: Tossed Back and Tempered by the Sea	111
Chapter 10: Frosted Patina	123
Chapter 11: Counterfeits	135
Chapter 12: Found from Reflection	147
Chapter 13: Intrinsic Value	163
References	179

Introduction

Robin Bertram said it best when she said, "The fires of refinement will shine the light of Christ into the dark places of our hearts, burn off the chaff, and restore us to a state of greater purity."[1] I have found that life is ever-changing and with those changes comes the removal of impurities God needs us to let go of.

I want nothing more than to see my siblings in Christ healed, whole, and thriving. Jeremiah 29:11 says, *"For I know the plans I have for you," declares the* LORD, *"plans to prosper you and not to harm you, plans to give you hope and a future."* If God already knows how much potential and how many good things are ahead of you, then let Him in. Let Him flood your soul with a warm ocean of purification. There is nothing that you have done or nothing others have done to you that will take away the good things He has for you.

Remember that your story is no surprise to Him. He's known every misstep and every destructive thought and behavior with which this life has shattered you. It's time, sweet reader, to let your creator pick up those pieces to finish your crafting. Any master crafter knows that it will take time to mold raw material such as gold into the adored jewelry that is showcased in the glass cabinet. Let Him file the edges and polish your heart, for you have value that needs to be displayed.

I hope that the pages that follow this Introduction will guide you into discovering who God has always wanted you to be. You'll find a journaling section with prompts at the end of every chapter to help you constructively dig into things within your heart.

With a rich background in ministry, I offer a fresh perspective on how to cultivate refinement in your life. I was dealt a hand that caused me to build a fortress around my heart. Over time I discovered that old wounds had threaded sharpness into my thoughts, responses, relationships with people, and ultimately my peace.

The Sea Glass Soul was birthed out of the ashes of one of my most trying times—divorce. During my time in counseling, I began to see that there were areas I needed to reach into. I didn't want to end up bitter or allow past hurts to cut into me yet again. I needed to know that before there was a broken relationship, there was a broken Jamie. I grew up having adult responsibilities placed on me at an early age. Things had to be taken care of, so that's what I did. But shame for not having a normal childhood crept in, and guilt for having transferred certain patterns of not trusting people or God dusted the feet of my marriage. It happened quietly—just like sand in the car after a day at the beach.

Despite all this, I found that things do need to wash ashore because only then can we see things as they really are. In other words, guilt, shame, and fear mixes with a lot of our

INTRODUCTION

experiences, which exacerbates all the yuck. I finally saw my worth the way God did the entire time; it just took a little while for me to see it.

I pray for the waves of healing to break through to show you all the beautiful pieces that have been churning in your ocean of hurt, waiting for you to discover them. No matter how stuck, damaged, or destroyed you think you might be, God has never left your side. Not even once.

CHAPTER 1

Forged by Fire

People and nations are forged in the fires of adversity.
— John Adams

It is often in our greatest brokenness that our greatest strengths are revealed to us. Glass isn't something that has always existed; it had to be formed—forged even. For centuries, well trained craftsmen formed beautiful glass objects such as sculptures, bottles, vases, and the list could go on.

One method used to create glass was called core forming. This technique was quite common in Egypt during biblical times. The core was made of mud; then the glass was formed around the mud mold. After a cooling period, the core-form was removed to reveal a hollow vessel that could be used as a person desired. As glassmaking evolved, core forming disappeared like heat waves on a cool Egyptian evening, and glassblowing was established.

Glassblowing had a more fine-tuned process and allowed for smaller furnaces to be used. Ancient artists took local materials and had them ground them into powder. The material usually included quartz, soda, lime, and finely crushed rocks; subsequently, these materials were mixed with grits of sand that craftsmen would then melt together. The artist would handle the molten glass using some sort of metal rod, which was spun centrifugally while the artist blew into the other end to expand the gills of the glass. And voilà, glass was formed.

Interestingly enough, the very thing that gave this ancient glass its color was its impurities.[2] Before I continue, let me pause to implore you as the sweet, beautiful soul that you are to know that all the things you wish were not in your life do not make you any less valuable in the eyes of the one who knit you together in your mother's womb. In the glassmaking process, "impurities" included various elements such as carbon, iron, gold, and rocks. Isn't it amazing how the crafters skillfully made something so beautiful from dust and impurities? The same God who gave these crafters ideas to create something from almost nothing can make something brand-new with your dust and impurities too.

In June 2023, I attended a glassblowing demonstration in the small town of Wimberly, Texas. It was a blistering Texas summer day with the mercury reading over 110 degrees. As the group moved from the glass gallery toward the workshop, I could feel the heat radiating through the door. I have no idea how the two glassblowers could withstand the heat for as long as they do. Because let me tell you, I was about ready for a second round of deodorant after a short time. That's how hot I was.

We made our way into the workshop and sat down in the middle of the bleachers. Tim, one of the artists, came over to us and began explaining various parts of his process. He said it was about 140 degrees on their side of the workshop where the furnace was.[3] Meanwhile, we were sitting at about 100 degrees. That day, they were making Father's Day cups; it was interesting to see the entire process from start to finish. The oven was a toasty little fireball sitting in the corner. You could be mesmerized by the bright amber glow of the flames, just as you might melt in peaceful relaxation watching the orange glow of a sunset.

Now by definition, glassblowing is the practice of shaping molten glass while blowing air into it through a stainless-steel tube called a blowpipe. The blowpipe is used to get the glass out of the furnace. In order for the glass to form correctly, the temperature within the furnace must be 2100 degrees Fahrenheit. That is an immensely high heat—far too extreme for human flesh to endure. Or so we think, sometimes.

Life has a way of bringing heat to us that feels too hot for us to bear on our own. I dare say that sometimes, the mere thought of being near severe heat deters us. Sooner or later though, we have to face the heat even when we don't want to. Much like the glass being shaped in the furnace, we have to allow the flames of life to shape us—to embrace the process and not run away from it.

In glassmaking, the temperature must be extremely intense; otherwise, the glass would never be soft enough to mold, shape, and become the masterpiece that the crafter desires it to be. We too can never be what our God desires us to be if we remain cold to the path designed for us.

On the other hand, if the furnace is too hot, the glass could burn up or explode. Certainly, God does not want us to explode either from the pressures that life throws at us. I do believe that He knows precisely how much heat we are able to withstand. He never promised we would have an easy journey on this side of Heaven, nor did He say we wouldn't be tempted by the things of this world meant to destroy us. Romans 8:18 says, *"For I reckon that the sufferings of this present time are not worthy to be compared with the glory which shall be revealed in us"* (KJV).

This brings me to a point about a phrase I often hear spoken when we are hard-pressed: "God isn't going to give you more than you can handle." Please know that this cliché is not biblical. He will allow whatever He deems necessary so that His great power can be shown in your life. He will also help you walk through every single situation even if it means picking you up because you have no more strength left to bear another step. You were never, ever, meant to do this life alone.

When the craftsman fills their lungs with air and releases it into the pipe, that same breath penetrates the glass, expanding the colors. The colors may begin as dark particles on top of molten glass, but as the elements expand together, the hues are seen more clearly. For example, blue particles look nearly black before the craftsman puts his breath to the pipe. However, when the glass stretches, a translucent blue is then illuminated to the eye. As the piece is formed, the steps in the process may not seem to make sense. The glass fluctuates and takes many forms before it takes its final shape. The artist's breath gives new life and form to what was previously just material.

Without that breath, it would still be nothing more than raw elements. Similarly, to be formed, we must be forged.

As I read about creation, the words from Scripture fill my soul: *"And the Lord God formed man of the dust of the ground, and breathed into his nostrils the breath of life; and man became a living being"* (Genesis 2:7 NKJV). We have the Lord's breath in us. He trusted us to be vessels to carry something so holy and important inside of us. That's how valuable and worthy we are to Him.

After the glass has withstood extreme heat and with much time and patience from the craftsman, it is taken out because the heat is only temporary. Temporary. Not lasting. The glass has an allotted amount of time in the fire and that is it. The heat ends. We do not serve under a cruel and ill-willed Father. As a good and caring father, He knows we must endure certain trials to grow. I would be a terrible parent if I did everything for my daughters and never allowed them to learn some things on their own.

When my youngest began playing softball, she struggled to hit the ball consistently. She began to grow frustrated with the change from hitting off a tee. It would have been quite silly to have her mama at home plate every game helping her bat and hit the ball. This struggle was necessary for her to persevere and strive to get better. I encouraged her that the key to getting better was a lot of practice and not giving up. It took about two months and a lot of pitches from Mom and her coach, but she finally got there. In fact, the first game they played she was the first one to get a base hit. She got there. She endured the struggle.

The book of Daniel shares a story about three men who faced a literal fire—being tossed into a fiery furnace by their king. He wanted to see if their God was real or a farce:

> *Shadrach, Meshach, and Abednego answered King Nebuchadnezzar, "Your threat means nothing to us. If you throw us in the fire, the God we serve can rescue us from your roaring furnace and anything else you might cook up, O king. But even if he doesn't, it wouldn't make a bit of difference, O king. We still wouldn't serve your gods or worship the gold statue you set up."*
>
> *Nebuchadnezzar, his face purple with anger, cut off Shadrach, Meshach, and Abednego. He ordered the furnace fired up seven times hotter than usual. He ordered some strong men from the army to tie them up, hands and feet, and throw them into the roaring furnace. Shadrach, Meshach, and Abednego, bound hand and foot, fully dressed from head to toe, were pitched into the roaring fire. Because the king was in such a hurry and the furnace was so hot, flames from the furnace killed the men who carried Shadrach, Meshach, and Abednego to it, while the fire raged around Shadrach, Meshach, and Abednego.*
>
> *Suddenly King Nebuchadnezzar jumped up in alarm and said, "Didn't we throw three men, bound hand and foot, into the fire?" "That's right, O king," they said.*

> *"But look!" he said. "I see four men, walking around freely in the fire, completely unharmed! And the fourth man looks like a son of the gods!"*
> —Daniel 3:16–25 MSG

There are lots of elements to look at here. I can only imagine the thoughts that were running through the minds of Shadrach, Meshach and Abednego. Yet, they were faithful and believed they would be taken care of. God not only made sure not a hair on their heads was singed, but he placed His son in the fire with them, so they were not alone. They came out 100 percent unharmed.

Think about the fires in your life. Yes, they're unconformable. Yes, we may feel the burning on the outside or the inside too sometimes. However, our souls are protected the whole time because God is in the midst of every fire in our lives protecting us even sometimes without us realizing it.

Dear sweet soul, if you stop reading after this sentence then so be it, but please hear me on this:

> The trials end.
> The depression fades.
> The abuse stops.
> The trauma gets reversed.
> The broken heart heals.
> The strongholds cease.
> The generational curses crumble.
> The financial struggles find favor.

All our trials are only for a season; do not think for one second that God has left you in your furnace alone or for forever. The cooling period comes. Wait for it; be patient and trust the process.

When the glass piece is removed from the heat, only then can the glass be shaped. Only after the heat of our life experiences is complete can we be shaped. Only then are we attentive and better able to listen; then we are adaptable and moldable just like the glass on the shaping table.

Here's this though: this process may have to be repeated more than a few times. The more intricate the design the maker has in mind, the more times the piece will have to endure the fire. As we watched Tim the glass crafter, he fired the glass many times to achieve the next step in his design. The piece needed ridges on the bottom, so he heated it up. It needed to be molded on the top for the rim, so he fired it up. Finally, he spun a special piece of glass and heated it up to create the handle for the mug. By the end of the demonstration, the once-raw materials had turned out to be a beautiful blue glass mug.

You, love, are intricate. You are not done yet. God loves you too much to let you be just "good enough" or just "OK." He wants you to be amazing because you are worth the time that He is willing to put into you. No, the steps don't always make sense, and the shape of the glass may change many times over. I look back over my life and see times when I was an impatient perfectionist. Now in my mid-thirties, one of my greatest compliments has been, "Jamie you're so patient." But oh, the fires I had to endure to get here. You didn't see my forging. You didn't see the impurities that had to come off and are still coming off. So no, my journey has not been easy.

Learning to take responsibility for my own actions, forgiving myself, and pushing through painful circumstances to allow myself to be molded has been excruciatingly difficult. Trust me, I fought the process every step of the way. I wanted to be the one in control of creating myself and my journey. I wanted to be the one to set the "done" timer, but I kept going around the mountain until I finally learned that was not the way.

The most beautiful thing about us and the Holy Spirit is that when our flames become one with the Spirit, we are unstoppable. That is the light the world needs to see, that it has to see. You must go through the fires, so you can be forged into the person you were meant to be. Glass, like iron, is never strong until it is heat-treated. If we had taken the mug home that day, Tim said it would have been in such a delicate state that it would have shattered easily. In the corner of the workshop was a special curing box in which all the items were placed so they could go through the process of annealing to relieve any internal stress fractures that formed as they were created. Miniscule fractures cause glass items to shatter; annealing resolves the fractures and makes the glass strong, durable, and stable. I certainly wouldn't want to put hot chocolate in the mug only to have the handle break off. Annealing is not a fast process; it took several hours for our mug to go through this process. So, we paid for shipping and handling and had our mug delivered the next week; we didn't want to mess up the process by being impatient to get the finished product.

Even with metals, heat and annealing makes the metal stronger and harder. But remember that the heat process is always controlled. The metal in our bridges can withstand hurricanes, earthquakes, and high winds because they are strong enough to stand up to the things of this world without being knocked down.

Dear reader, you are strong enough to stand up without wavering while having the purity to shine. Scripture assures us:

> *Pure gold put in fire comes out of it proved pure; genuine faith put through this suffering comes out proved genuine. When Jesus wraps this all up, it's your faith, not your gold, that God will have on display as evidence of his victory.*
>
> —1 Peter 1:7 MSG

For gold refining, the controlled heat is between 1,830–2,150 degrees Fahrenheit. Too little heat does nothing; too much heat ruins the integrity of the element. Just the right amount of heat causes the impurities to surface. As they do, a craftsman scrapes them off, applies the next increment of heat until all the impurities have surfaced and been removed.

A lot of things seem unfair, unkind, and out of balance when it comes to the cards we're dealt. I don't believe that things that happen to you are God's fault. They come out of a very broken world in which we live and the free will or capacity of other people. Nevertheless, God has overseen every single second. He has been there with you and still knows how it's going to play out. I have found that He can make something beautiful from it all—even the things that are awful—if we give Him the broken pieces.

God allows one increment of heat at a time to remove our impurities, so that we are refined according to His image. Every person is unique and requires a different purification of the heart to rid us of things this world, others, or ourselves have put there over time. For example, our hearts may have been defiled by sin and negativity from negative life experiences and environments we have been exposed to. Such impurities need to be removed if we are to grow or be forged spiritually.

To be forged means to be created. We are formed into who the Lord wants us to be as we go through difficult seasons; according to God's design, the process removes our impurities. But the process requires obedience and consistency on our part through prayer and reading the word to put the Lord's love into our hearts. It's also done by sometimes seeking counsel on matters in which we need accountability or wisdom. Finally, we must be willing to mature in our emotional responses to ourselves and others. If the goldsmith turned off the heat in the middle of forging the impurities, what would happen? The gold would still have some of the junk in it, correct? In similar fashion, God applies consistent heat in our lives for a long as it takes to remove certain impurities.

I will let you into my world for a moment. Teenager rearing is rough—probably rougher than the terrible twos or trying threes. I always thought to myself, "I have a community of people over in the distance to help, but I will be fine. I was a youth pastor for six and a half years, so I have a ton of experience handling teenagers." My goodness . . . was I wrong! I feel like whatever you think you know about raising a teen, you just toss it out the window during a hurricane and then the flood waters are going to take that book and turn it back into paper pulp. Along with that feeling, I am grieving the girl she once was, wading in the waters of transition, suffering post-divorce grief, and moving into a season of understanding the young woman she's becoming.

There have been tears—oh my word, the tears! Tears at work, on my way home, over the phone, middle of the night, and so on. God has seen my heartbroken sorrow as a mother intimately. Psalm 56:8 says, *"You keep track of all my sorrows. You have collected all my tears in your bottle. You have recorded each one in your book"* (NLT). I think He's probably got a whole shelf filled with bottles labeled, "Jamie's Tears." This process has humbled me to see things as He sees them as a parent.

I have prayed for years that the Lord would give me the eyes He has for his people. Little did I know fifteen years later, I was going to be seeing those prayers come to life. Looking back, I see and feel all the times that I was the one with the rebellious spirit or being disrespectful to my parents. I also remember being in seasons of disobedience with God. I was wanting to do my own thing, yet I was breaking His big papa heart at the same time. I can imagine my mother and father shared God's frustrations. My mama heart understands now.

Instead of thinking I just had my village on reserve, I feel like I have been in constant contact with them, sometimes daily. This stage of child-rearing is hard and quite frankly sucks. But I can tell you this; it is necessary for my daughter's forging and mine as well. Though I felt like I was already humble, I needed some more refinement. Or at least the God thought so. I felt like I was decently strong, but I needed to allow God to replace more pillars in my heart to cast them His way.

Through it all, I have prayed, worshipped, and leaned in closer to God like I never have before. There were lessons I needed to learn. I needed to pray consistently, instead of relying on a one-and-done prayer. I anointed my home with oil instead of believing it was a religious act, and I sought counsel and healed myself instead of keeping it all in and having the pent-up emotions seep out. There is no comparison for a mother or parent who is brokenhearted over their children and wails in the night for them. If my hallway walls could talk, they'd tell you the multitude of times I was on the floor praying with hot tears pouring off like a summer storm.

We do not know what the future holds or what the outcome will be. Much like how the glass doesn't know what it will be forged into, but the Master Crafter does, and that's all that matters.

Chapter 1 Journal Prompts

1. What fires in life do you feel have shaped you into who you are? (Write down positive ways and negative ways. You're just writing down events/circumstances/thoughts here, not the how's.)

2. How has the heat of life's circumstances affected you and the environments around you? (Write down things like this: *It made me feel this; when xyz happens like it did in these situations, I tend to xyz with my thoughts, words, or actions; I recognize pattern xyz, so now I do xyz, which feels good.* Explore the positive and negatives here. Get into a place where you can let your pen flow freely. Don't worry about putting it into sentences, and don't over think it. Whatever your first thoughts are, write those down.)

3. What are positive things you'd like to achieve from journaling through this book?

CHAPTER 2

Carafes

Whatever God has given us; we are just the vessel for it.
—Clayton Kershaw

A carafe is a glass container without handles; it is commonly used to serve wine, juice, or other drinks. In restaurants, servers use carafes to pour water or other beverages into your glass. Interestingly enough, the shape of the carafe doesn't change the quality or taste of the liquid it contains; it is merely a vessel, a container. The liquid in a carafe retains its characteristics. A carafe may be plain or have an intricate design pressed into the seamless glass; some have stains of color while remaining transparent. Most of the ones I see are clear; however, some are done in colors that resemble the ocean's deep opaque shadows.

Carafes are inanimate objects; whereas we are living, breathing humans, but one thing holds true of us both. Both carafes and humans are vessels that hold something for our bodies to consume. Carafes hold delicious beverages for our bodies that entice our taste buds, or they may hold the life-giving element of water. Similarly, once we establish a relationship with Jesus, God packs us full of many good things. Some are elements we'll need for life to flow freely from us, so we can nurture ourselves and others around us. He becomes the "living water" inside us, and He enables us to establish well-watered ground for our hearts to grow new things and maintain our lives as we mature in Christ.

During His ministry, Jesus came to Samaria and stopped at Jacob's well. While He was at the well, a Samaritan woman came to draw water. Please note that this happened in the middle of the day, which means it was very hot—not the time of day when most people came to draw water. The woman felt that midday was the best time for her to come, given that she had a promiscuous past and did not want to shame herself publicly. It is also important to note that the writer points out that Jews and Samaritans did not associate with each other (John 4:9). However, Jesus did not discriminate. He was for all people, not just the Jews. John 4:13–19 (NKJV) records His conversation with the woman at the well:

> *Jesus answered and said to her, "Whoever drinks of this water will thirst again, but whoever drinks of the water that I shall give him will never thirst. But the water that I shall give him will become in him a fountain of water springing up into everlasting life.*
>
> *The woman said to Him, "Sir, give me this water, that I may not thirst, nor come here to draw."*

> *Jesus said to her, "Go, call your husband, and come here."*
>
> *The woman answered and said, "I have no husband."*
>
> *Jesus said to her, "You have well said, 'I have no husband,' for you have had five husbands, and the one whom you now have is not your husband; in that you have spoken truly."*
>
> *The woman said to Him, "Sir, I perceive that You are a prophet."*

As you can see in this passage, when the woman says that she has no husband, Jesus does not shame her; He simply acknowledges the truth of what she has said. He gave her grace because she confessed her sin first. He also delivers the message that He is her living water; He didn't want her to thirst for the things of the world ever again.

I also think he wanted to drive this point home to us because later in the book of John, he talks about living water again. In that instance, Jesus and His disciples were at a festival when He promised living water to the crowds:

> *On the last and greatest day of the festival, Jesus stood and said in a loud voice, "Let anyone who is thirsty come to me and drink. Whoever believes in me, as Scripture has said, rivers of living water will flow from within them." By this he meant the Spirit, whom those who believed in him were later to receive. Up to that time the Spirit had not been given, since Jesus had not yet been glorified.*
>
> —John 7:37–39

Being a carafe is not a bad thing in and of itself. In addition to the living water that Jesus supplies us, we may function as carafes for different relationships, experiences, joy, death, or even hurts. As a mother, I hold nurture, care, provision, safety, and guidance for my children—things that they will need throughout their lives. I have allowed myself to be a vessel the Lord can pour into, so I can pour into my daughters.

The Bible gives us this example in 2 Timothy 2:21: *"Therefore, if anyone cleanses himself from what is dishonorable, he will be a vessel for honorable use, set apart as holy, useful to the master of the house, ready for every good work"* (ESV). You, sweet reader, are no different. If the Lord believes all these things about you, please accept them. The creator of the universe loves you so much that He sent His one and only son to die on the cross just for you:

> You are clean.
> You are useful.
> You are worthy of good things.
> You are capable of being exactly who you are.

Let's consider pitchers for a moment. They can hold beverages that are beneficial to our overall well-being, such as water or green tea. But pitchers can also be used to hold large amounts of alcohol or other substances that can be detrimental and cause our bodies to fail from various ailments. Picture a clear glass pitcher full of pure, clean water. You can see straight through it because there is nothing in it to distort images or corrupt the pure water inside. It is free of debris, rocks, soil, or impurities.

In some ways, you can think of your heart as a "pitcher," which is greatly affected by the things put into it. Oftentimes, the world, the enemy, or we ourselves pack unhealthy things into our "pitcher," such as actions or thoughts that cause us to sin or hold onto other people's junk that we harbor in our hearts. Think of each impurity as being equivalent to a spoonful of dirt. The impurities I have in mind include half-truths, self-doubt, anxiety, or negative thinking. They may also include things we pick up from others such as conflict, insecurities, and excessive anger—one spoonful of dirt at a time. All these things can soil our perceptions even further and before you know it, the clear water in our pitcher would look cloudy and repulsive.

If our metaphorical pitchers were seen by you or others in such a contaminated state, would you drink that water? Would you give that to your children? Would you serve that to guests you invited to your home? Better yet, would you serve that to your heavenly King? You most definitely would not. Over time though this is how our hearts look when we allow all the yuck to be spooned in. It's never done all at once either; we get filled up with one spoonful, one experience, one thought, and one word at a time.

Finally, the "pitcher" gets filled to the brim with dirt and water, and the contents spill over when the pitcher is moved. This is what happens when our hearts are full of yuck and we try to go from one relationship to another. Or even one workplace to another or one season of life to another. All the junk inside spills over into each area of our lives and onto others too. I don't believe we intentionally mean to spill over the yuck, but sometimes it happens when we're not emotionally regulated or in a healthy mindset.

The junk affects the way we respond to others. Maybe you didn't mean to say something in a harsh or hurtful way, but other people's reaction to what you said sets off a chain of unintended consequences. The other person's reaction may be defensive, offended, angry, or sad; sometimes the relationship with that person may become irreparable. For example, if I come to work with a frustrated heart because I am feeling overwhelmed with deadlines or stress that others have poured onto me, I may feel overstimulated. I remember a time when this happened. I walked into work and hadn't set my coffee on the desk when someone approached me requesting information from me immediately. I responded in a negative sarcastic tone—in a not so nice way. Feelings were hurt, and I felt guilty for responding the way that I did. But my "pitcher" was full of not so good things, and it unfortunately seeped out unfairly onto a coworker. When we read God's word and work on ourselves and engage in an intimate relationship with Jesus, living water is poured into our pitcher. The momentum of the water pouring in forces the junk out. And the more we repeat this process, the more the junk floats out of the pitcher—out of our hearts.

So, what if a little more of that junk pours out? It's OK. So, what if you're starting over at fortysomething? It's OK. So, what if you messed up and you have to do something over again? It's OK. And what if you were doing so good fighting that battle only you and God know about, but you fall into old patterns and mess up . . . again? It is OK.

Let's take it a step further. Take the pitcher and fill it with rocks. Every rock represents what we think of as the heavier things, such as addictions, intrusive thoughts, rage, depression, and so many of the weighty things that are meant to destroy us. To break us. If these are allowed to stay inside, the weight might be too much for a glass carafe or pitcher. It has a delicate nature not intended to bear such contents. Perhaps the "rocks" would fracture the glass, thus shattering the bottom. Or worse yet, the rocks might cause scratches as they scrape against the inside of the structure, gradually fracturing the once pristine vessel.

If a pitcher is something that holds a drink safely, then what happens if it topples off a counter and shatters? The contents will be scattered everywhere once the vessel is broken. A new pitcher will be needed. The beautiful thing about carafes is that, even if they break, the stuff on the inside is what is most important. The carafe is what holds the valuable things safe. Our body is what keeps our soul safe. Sure, it may get tumbled around a bit, maybe even bruised, but it is always safe.

For the good things to come back in, we must allow for the breaking, so the yuck can come out. Only then can we have a stronger, wiser, more mature self. What's inside us is valuable. Why else do you think both God and Satan are after it? 1 Peter 2:11 declares this for us, *"Dear friends, your real home is not here on earth. You are strangers here. I ask you to keep away from all the sinful desires of the flesh. These things fight to get hold of your soul"* (NLV).

The more the enemy can get you distracted, discouraged, tempted, and redirected, the more he paves the way for your actions to become sinful. We undermine ourselves, which is what the enemy wants, but he provides the opportunity or tools for us to advance our sinful nature. Don't praise him accidentally by giving him all the credit. I have done that with ease for many years. Hold your praise for the testimony of your God who will be faithful to get you out of your messes.

This is exactly why Scripture tells us to keep our hearts safe. God delivered a message to us in the Old Testament, urging us to be careful: *"Keep your heart with all vigilance, for from it flow the springs of life"* (Proverbs 4:23 ESV). You have been given authority over your enemies, but you must not let your heart be tainted with things meant to destroy you. If you do, it will seep into your life like a sticky tarlike substance, which is nearly impossible to clean. Or the effects may be like fragments of glass when a pitcher breaks into thousands of shards, which can embed themselves in the most miniscule of areas.

Something I have struggled with more than you will ever know, is letting God take control. I am a planner and organizer by default. In fact, anytime a family member or friend needs a party planned, I'm the one on speed-dial. I once planned a party for my niece with only three days' notice. I am also a mom and a volunteer at church and other organizations. Many times, I have been asked to lead and take over planning or implement manuals for future programs. I am also responsible for planning ahead for my full-time job, my daughter's extracurricular activities, and whatever else may be in our path.

Sometimes, I am tempted to do things my way instead of God's way. When things get messy, I end up coming to his altar saying, "I'm sorry I made this mess. Please help me clean it up." The ironic thing is I know He will help me with everything in my life. I know He will help me with the details. I just so badly want to work on all of them myself.

During one of my sessions with my counselor, I realized how much I was questioning His ability to help me with everything. The root of it was not believing that He was going to come through for me. A wounded part of me still needed to be acknowledged and healed. I was used to taking care of everything for everyone because that was how I coped with the void in my heart when I was younger. It was hard to trust and believe that someone would take care of me emotionally, mentally, spiritually, and physically. What if they left? What if they died? What was I to do? Would God always be there for me? Even now, I sometimes struggle with the idea of things falling apart.

God is most definitely in the business of proving me wrong though. When I think He's going to fall through, He always shows up. It feels like one of those crazy trust exercises that I do not like to engage in. The thought of trust exercise exacerbates the anxiousness in my mind. Then I hear the Spirit saying something like this:

> Jamie, I really can take care of you. I really do know what I'm doing over here. But OK sure, you don't trust me yet; that's all right. We'll take the long way this time if that's what's needed. I'm patient. I'll wait. I know this is hard for you. Just know when you feel the weight of everything coming on you and you're humbly in a place to allow me to help then I will. I'm here. Just say when.

That's what I love so much about God. He never pushes us into His plans, and His grace extends far beyond what my heart can comprehend. He is the best gentleman I have ever known. I like to think that every time I take my blueprint of all my plans to Him, He takes it, smiles, and says:

> I see what you'd like to have. This is your best. Your best in the natural world. Your best in your own ability. Your best in what you think you deserve. But oh, sweet child of mine, I am the supernatural and sovereign God. Will you allow Me to do My best? Will you allow Me to act in My supernatural ability to do signs and wonders in your life that will be a part of your story woven into Mine? Will you let me show you what you really do deserve according to My riches and My glory and let Me do on earth what I have already stored up for you in Heaven?

You may not always get what you want, but He is always going to deliver what you need. Being a carafe or a vessel is not a bad thing in and of itself. We are forged, yet we can break just as easily as glass. At the end of the day or at the end of our existence this side of Heaven, we may be broken or bruised, but our sweet and precious souls are always safe.

Chapter 2 Journal Prompts

1. What kinds of things are you holding in your heart? (We're naming things here and identifying what we, others, or the enemy have put in your heart that don't need to be there.)

2. How has your "pitcher" spilled over into other areas of your life?

3. What are some positive ways you've allowed God to remake you?

CHAPTER 3

Broken Pieces and Sharp Edges

Your brokenness is not a deterrent to God's purpose.
—Toby Mac

This is the breaking part. The part that hurts. The part that we wish wouldn't have happened. It's the part that makes me want to flip past this chapter and skip to the last chapter. However, it would be a complete disservice to you and me if we looked away from the vulnerable places of our hearts. That is where our connection and understanding can grow within ourselves and with God and others. Brené Brown says it best in her book, *The Gifts of Imperfection*: "We cultivate love when we allow our most vulnerable and powerful selves to be deeply seen and known."[4]

My sweet, beautiful friend, I know that the pain you have endured has been a heavy burden to carry. I have found that we women are strong, but perhaps we carry so much because we feel we have to. If you're like me, you've carried burdens you shouldn't have—things that were put on you by your family, your own ideals, friends, and even past or current relationships.

We would like to carry it all and say at the end of the day, "Take that, world, I did this; I carried this today." But how does that make you feel? Are your shoulders worn down? Are you exhausted? If you aren't yet, you may be very soon. The burdens we carry sometimes stem from a prideful place or from situations we regret being in.

I am by far the worst at carrying things I shouldn't. For a very long time, I was the girl and later the woman, who always answered with the infamous phrase, "I'm fine." This phrase makes everyone think, "Oh she's totally got this . . . wow look at her. Jamie can handle everything." I can't even begin to tell you how many times I have said that in my lifetime. Correct me if I'm wrong, but I'm sure that you have said, "I'm fine," when, on the inside, you are saying something much darker. Perhaps your inner thoughts are saying: "I am struggling but I'm embarrassed to say. I am so hurt, but I can't express it because of past hurts. I am exhausted; I just need a break. I don't know what to do with this situation, but if I talk about it, then people will think that I'm weak."

Honestly, you and I both know that list could fill many pages, so I'll stop there for now. For Christian women, it is incredibly easy to say we are OK when, in fact, we are truly not. What a lie we have learned to tell ourselves. Perhaps it was what we learned to protect ourselves from the world, so it would seem a little less scary. Maybe we've always been strong because we felt we had to. Or maybe your story is even different from that. Maybe you've lived in what I'll call the "expected feminine masculinity" of yourself because you didn't have a healthy male figure in your life. That is, you became a strong, independent woman capable of performing both feminine and masculine roles even though this wasn't the design for your life. You did it because you felt you had to fill both roles in your life because you didn't have strong feminine and masculine role models when you were a child. Trying to fill both roles may be acceptable—even unavoidable—for the short term, but it is not sustainable, nor does it lead to a fulfilling lifestyle. I found myself fixing things, working full time, tending to kids, and running them everywhere. I was burning myself out rapidly, and so will you if you're on a similar path. Yes, short term that is OK to do to get things done.

When I was ten years old, my mother became very ill, and the doctors did not know the reason for her illness. She is still with us today, but those were hard times—times when I cried myself to sleep because I didn't know if my mom was going to be alive in the morning. I felt anxious not knowing our future as a family. Who would take care of us if Mom passed away? Would Dad be all right? What about all the bills they talked about? What would life look like without her? Would I be able to carry this weight on my shoulders?

My younger brother was seven or eight at the time and before long, I had the dual role of being big sister and mom to him. I needed to help him with homework, and meals needed to be made, and other chores required attention. My weekly morning routine consisted of waking up at five in the morning, making our lunches, getting breakfast ready, and giving my mom a shot in her upper thigh—all before the school bus picked us up. I had to attend her doctors' appointments and learn how to administer an experimental drug in her leg. The thought of doing this frightened me, but I was the only one available for the task.

When she reached a critical stage in her sickness, I also had to monitor and disburse her feeding tube supplements. Her nutritional needs were not being met due to her condition, so a feeding tube was the only way that she could get nourishment into her body. Unfortunately, anything that she ate by mouth would either not stay down, or she would experience severe abdominal pain.

It certainly wasn't my mother's fault that she wasn't able to function as the mom she wanted to be. Being a mom myself, I know it was hard on her physically and emotionally that she was not healthy enough to do things for us. How difficult it must have been for her, wanting to be with her children for field days, special occasions, and even walks in the park, but not being able to do so. I remember the last time she took us to a park and played basketball with us before her illness set in. I remember the last vacation we took as a family too. We didn't know it would be our last. I also saw my father support my mother through every treatment, every doctor's appointment—even when the doctors would say, "Well this didn't work, and we don't know why. We don't know what to do." I am very blessed to have had a father with such a caring heart.

I remember at one point, doctors were so dumbfounded by her worsening condition and failed treatments, they suggested that the illness was all in her head. They believed her pain was phantoms of her mind taunting her. Can you imagine your doctor saying such a thing?

Years have gone by since those raw moments of uncertainty. I have a newfound appreciation for my mom and the excruciating years she survived. Pressing pause for a moment in this story, I need you to understand that God did not create pain or suffering. That was 100 percent from the broken world we live in. It was allowed this side of Heaven, but it is not something God ever initially intended us to endure.

Back to my point, the pain we experience in life may cause breaking within us. Some of that breaking is from the hurt put on us by events, others, accidents, and, yes, even ourselves. Whether it is physical, mental, or spiritual pain, it is still pain, and it all hurts just the same. It may be extended over lengthy periods of time, or it may come in short waves. I cannot tell you when it will end, but I do know that it is only for a season.

When glass breaks, we often see giant chunks flying off into the air. We say some choice words if we're injured by flying glass or if the object was something we really did not want to break. After a moment of insanity caused by our flustered emotional state, we typically walk out frustrated and prepare to clean up the debris. We'll grab a broom and return to the place of brokenness. The mess will look up at us from the floor, and we'll sweep up the pieces of something that used to be whole. Something that used to be what we thought was complete.

Finally, we'll discard the mess into the garbage and on the day of our pick-up service, we will have forgotten all about the incident. Until we're walking barefoot across the floor and feel an itty-bitty, devilish piece of glass pierce our skin. It may even spill blood onto a freshly mopped floor.

Guess what happens next. We get upset, and the whole entire incident of breaking something replays in our minds. We'll say more choice words about how we can't believe we didn't see that little piece of glass. All the while, we are bandaging our wound trying to remember our Girl Scout skills from twenty years prior.

The giant chunks of pain, the parts that come off when something happens, are usually the things we can deal with first. It's those little needle-like shards that we can't see or forget about that will get us every time. Maybe not at first, but eventually, pain from something will creep back in and remind us, in effect, saying, "Hey, I'm still here; you haven't dealt with me yet. You want to deal with it today, like right now? How about in an hour or two? Oh wait, I know . . . how about right before bedtime; let's do that! I'll see you later!"

Sometimes, the broken pieces that are left hidden are a bit bigger than shards. They may represent a chunk of brokenness inside us that has memory. It remembers all the junk, the details, the conversations, the experience, the shame, and the "how-could-they" statements. These are the pieces that have sharp edges; these pieces keep cutting and are different from the shards. The shards we can pull out over time with some tweezers and a little bit of antibiotic ointment.

The chunks, however, are harder to extract. It will take skill, surgery (if the chunks are deeply embedded), and most likely stiches to close the wound left from extraction. As if this isn't enough, this procedure will most likely leave a scar, which will be a little reminder of what happened from the sharp edge of the glass that sliced your skin. Even though we know it's necessary to get the chunks of pain out, it is an excruciatingly painful process.

If we don't remove the chunks, we risk infection, which could lead to other problems. This could include sepsis, which is a dire blood infection caused by our body being in overdrive to heal. We also risk having pieces of glass split off into smaller ones. When this happens, our pain can break off into bitterness, unforgiveness, or even a hardened heart—all of which are completely unhealthy to us but also to other people.

Years ago, glassmakers came up with a tempering process that would prevent glass from shattering upon impact. This process is used to manufacture glass used in vehicle windshields and windows. Upon a hard impact, the tempered glass shatters in place and can then be removed in a sheet instead of millions of pieces. Unfortunately, I know what it's like to be in a car accident and have seen firsthand what this looks like. The experience was unpleasant, destructive, and traumatic. At the ripe young age of 16, I drove my family's only vehicle to a friend's house to borrow a specific color of nail polish I just "had to have." Pulling up to the end of our street, I looked both ways like any good driver does. To my left I saw a vehicle parked at the gas station as the driver waited for a safe moment to turn onto the busy highway. However, I assumed the way was clear for me, turned left, and pulled right in front an older gentleman driving a pickup truck.

This was the biggest vehicle accident I had ever been in. My vehicle spun around several times, and when it came to a stop, my parents' SUV was facing the opposite direction. Glass was shattered, airbags were inflated, and one very freaked-out teenager was in the driver's seat. Thankfully, my dad wasn't too upset since I wasn't injured severely. I was grounded, not for the accident, but for not paying attention and for assuming rather than basing my decision to pull onto the road on facts. Although the glass was broken, it was merely shattered across one large surface. The police officer on scene told me that the accident could have been much worse. Glass could have been broken and lodged in different parts of my body. However, that was not the case. Because the glass in our car had been tempered, it did its job and kept me safe from further injury.

Sometimes, God allows shattering, but we remain unscathed. Situations can feel devastating in the moment, traumatic even. But what if. . . What if the reason you were held in a tempering season was so that when the shattering season comes, *you* won't be shattered. Instead, only the things around you shatter. And what if after some time of healing from the devastation of the event, you realize that the whole process was to keep you from further destruction even though it was difficult to endure.

Don't forget that, within those broken pieces that fell off from your life, there is a certain beauty that can come from the sharp edges. They can be tamed; they can be smoothed out. Healing is the product of pieces being released from our hurting hearts. Isaiah 43:19 says, *"See; I am doing a new thing! Now it springs up; do you not perceive it? I am making a way in the wilderness and streams in the wasteland."* When the vessel breaks in ways we think it shouldn't, perhaps it's not the vessel's undoing; rather it's the beginning of a new thing.

I'm going to be honest; I didn't want to write this chapter. So much so that I skipped over it to write others first. I stopped writing early last winter, and it is now mid-March. Knowing the gentle side of God, I understood that He knew that was what I needed to do. He knew that I needed time and space to heal and sort through some stuff. The Holy Spirit has been nudging me to pen the rest of this chapter for months now. I came out to the seaside, ready to write encouraging, uplifting words. You know the kind I'm taking about—those neatly presented words fashioned into a feel good warm and fuzzy chapter. It's not that kind of chapter though.

When I come to the seashore, I like it to be peaceful not only in my surroundings but also in my spirit. Lately, my spirit has been heavy—almost in a pushing me down to the ground kind of way. In the same way, I've learned that if I do not sit with aloneness, fear, and anxiety, then I'm not really healing. All I'm doing is shoving it in the laundry basket, pushing it into my dark closet, and leaving it to just sit there. I know in my head that those clothes aren't going to move from that place until I take the time to put them away properly.

In the same way, until we heal properly, pain will still be in our heart closets waiting for us to deal with it. So, I was finally ready to resume writing this chapter. With waves beckoning my attention, I unpacked my brown leather portfolio, my pen, and my coffee and walked along the shore. I found two pieces of sea glass—one small green one and one arrowhead-shaped frosted white one.

Each piece has started to take on the transformation process from broken to beautiful and being turned into a treasured piece of sea glass. They both have jagged edges—so jagged that they'd probably slice my skin if dragged across it. The edges don't mirror the smoothness that finished pieces have. The surface has begun the frosted patina process, but it has much further to go. They need to be tossed back into the sea so that it can temper them. Until we allow our broken pieces to soften and be smoothed out, they will continue to cut into every other part of us and others.

When I took a break from writing this chapter it was because I had this strange writer's block. I just couldn't seem to finish the rest of the details, and it felt all jumbled up in my head. Truly the season reflected the state of my heart. I wasn't 100 percent broken yet, even though I thought I was. How in the world could I write the rest of this chapter without allowing the process to be completed? It was like I was trying to catch a plate in slow motion as it was crashing to the floor. Except the plate was me. I was stressed to the max with my full-time job, trying to be a mom, taking college courses, and trying to be on top of everything. Be "strong" was my mantra; I was surface leveling my anxiety and staying in things I knew I needed to let go of.

I was nearing what I thought was my max. Little did I know that physically I had passed it. My body was about to throw me a severe check engine light. Knowing I needed a break, I booked a camping trip for my kids and me thinking, "I just need to change my scenery for a bit." I needed to get away from it all because I just knew that I knew that I knew . . . this was the solution. However, all the way to the campground, I kept feeling off. I was dizzy; my heart would not stop pounding, and I could feel my blood pressure was in a dire state. Half of my face had intermittent twitching, and I felt like I couldn't catch my breath.

My girls and I unpacked the truck, took a hike, but I still was feeling off. I took my blood pressure; it was at an extremely high level, which compounded the entire situation and made my heart race even more. All I could think about was if I have a heart attack and die, what is going to happen to my girls? There is no one here with us. I'm three and a half hours from home; I can't traumatize them like that. I grew up with a sick parent, and I did not want my kids to have to experience that.

I kept my composure with the girls, and I went to the restroom to have a private prayer with the Lord. I said, "If you give me a second chance, then I promise to drop anything or anyone in my life that is going to hinder my relationship with you. If it is not in line with your purpose for me, take it or them away and give me the strength to do so."

It's not that I didn't know what I needed to do; I did. I was just scared. All the what-ifs played in my mind and then came the "but God" rationalizations. I came to a very humble state of mind and decided to call my ex-husband to come and get the girls. I did not want to do that, but I knew that would be the best and wisest choice for them if something were to happen to me.

I came home and went straight to my primary care physician for an examination. Her diagnosis surprised my worried heart. She said, "It's just anxiety; take these two anti-anxiety medications and within a few days, you'll find that you feel better." Two days later, I could not get a sense of normalness within my body. Surely, I thought to myself something is seriously wrong for me to still be feeling this way. The prognosis I received earlier in the week must be incorrect, I reasoned.

The next day, I went to work for half of the day, but I could not focus on anything I was doing; my mind felt foggy. My boss told me to take the rest of the week off and try to relax. I drove myself home and sat in the hammock next to my horse pasture.

Hundreds of thoughts were racing through my mind as I lay there feeling unhopeful. I dosed off in hopes of prayers being answered to make me feel well magically. To my disappointment, that did not happen. Hours passed and another night of being alone was nearing. Flares of anxiousness were begging for my attention; then I felt pain fluttering in my chest. Was this it? Was something detrimental about to transpire?

I went to the emergency room where they did an EKG, checked my blood pressure, did a chest x-ray, and ran various blood tests to check my body for signs of a heart attack. Good or bad, I wanted tangible proof of something being shown. The doctor came into the room to read off the results. The final verdict? Everything was normal. The diagnosis was again just anxiety. I asked, "Are you sure? What about all the physical symptoms I was experiencing?" They told me, "Yes ma'am, we are sure." Evidently, a panic attack can feel similar to a heart attack. My body was getting stuck in fight-or-flight mode. I was told to rest and not do anything for the remainder of the week. This also meant I had to take more time off work and lean into certain people that I did not want to. Anyone who is close to me can tell you that it is very hard for me to not do things or to sit still. My mind constantly thinks and is moving me along to the next thing to do.

There I was, scared things were going to be detrimental, anxious to sleep because you know the whole what-if thing. I was worried that the problem was more than just anxiety, and I was embarrassed and angry that my body had failed me. I was even upset with God and thought, "All I have to do is just sit around and rest? Really?"

At first, I hated it and then slowly as the week crawled on, I learned to embrace the slower pace. It was a reality check—a reminder that I absolutely could not do all the things all the time. I needed to cut some people out, live a healthier lifestyle, and trim my schedule down drastically. I also needed to have a deeper relationship with Jesus and learn the true meaning of rest and resting well. The other lie I was believing was that I didn't believe I was worthy of rest. My lifestyle centered on working hard and pushing forward. Down to the very core of my soul, I knew that my whole life depended on this change. In this extremely raw and broken state, I knew I was right where I needed to be and that my true healing was beginning.

The weekend was nearly over and as the sun set, I reflected on the events of that week. Hard conversations were had—some with myself, some with others, and many with the Lord. One conversation truly broke my heart, and I wept for months over it. I knew space was needed, but I didn't want this person out of my life forever. Their friendship had meant the world to me, but it was time to navigate the seas without them. I had to put my full trust in the Lord to believe that He knew what He was doing even though I didn't. The night before I went back to work, the Holy Spirit kept whispering to me to let go of the fears.

I crumpled to the floor in the doorway of my bedroom and wept for hours. I didn't want to be a prisoner of my anxiety and fear any longer. Scriptures I had tucked away in my heart began to surface in my memory as I gained a refreshed peace. For the first time in a very long time, I began to speak in tongues for what seemed like hours. His peace washed over my soul like a warm breeze on a spring seaside day. After this, I truly believed that the Lord had delivered me from my anxiety. I was tired but I didn't feel exhausted. I felt the stronghold of fear leave my home and my body. I didn't physically feel bound by distress anymore. God showed up in the middle of my mess. He needed me to be alone, so I would fully listen. He needed me to not stubbornly rely on my own strength so that I could lean into His. He had to do it. He had to deliver me so He could get the glory for it.

We have the propensity to toss aside what we think is broken, destroyed, confusing, and misunderstood. What I have found is that brokenness equals healing. How could we ever expect healing to come unless we allow ourselves to break completely so that God can put us together in a new way. His way. Yes, it's a process, and yes, it is incredibly hard. It's the only way though.

Sweet reader, if He has calmed your seas and your storms, then what is there to be afraid of? The waters are safe. He really will do what His word says. God is always ready to offer peace when we have to the eyes and the heart to accept it.

Without pain there is not the genuine authenticity of healing. Just like sea glass, it's OK to have both broken edges and soft ones at the same time.

Chapter 3 Journal Prompts

To allow hearts to be molded into the best versions of ourselves, we must acknowledge and examine these broken pieces. I know that it's uncomfortable, and I really wish there was a way to have chocolate ice cream make everything all better. But alas, that's not the way the real world works. We have to get into the nitty-gritty details if we want those things to come out of our hearts.

Broken Pieces and Sharp Edges

Before you start this section of journaling, stop and pray. Pray that the Lord will give you the capacity to search your heart for the things that have shattered it, cut into it, or cut into others. Invite the Holy Spirit into your inner self to wash ashore what needs to be healed.

1. What parts of your inner self do you feel are the pieces you need to look at?

2. What kinds of rough edges do they have? Are they jagged or pointy? Do they cut into others or yourself from your words or actions? Perhaps some edges have smoothed out but there are a few things that need to be deburred. These could show up as rough attitudes, the way you say things to people or the way you talk to yourself. Be descriptive here about the form these rough edges have taken in your life.

3. Now that you have acknowledged these broken pieces, what caused them to be there? What do they stem from? How far back is their origin? Prayerfully take your time to work through this section. You may find, as you begin to search for answers, that the broken places may cause pain or triggering. Allow yourself as much time as you need to journal in this section. I like to find a quiet place without distractions and let my pen flow on the pages. I don't worry about sentence structure or putting all your thoughts together cohesively. I encourage you to find your peaceful place to journal and to write whatever comes to mind on your paper.

4. You've identified some pieces of discomfort, so let's dive a little deeper into them. Did someone else's pain end up hurting you by their words or actions? Were the broken pieces put there by you? If any pieces still have rough edges, do you feel as though it's because they offer a sense of protection? What's your fear if they were smoothed out?

CHAPTER 4

The Sea

The heart of man is very much like the sea, it has its storms, it has its tides and, in its depths, it has its pearls too.

—Vincent van Gogh

Being a Texas Gulf Coast resident, the sea has been my neighbor my entire life. It is common to see bumper stickers that say "Salt Water Soul." For many, the sea provides a way of life whether from boating, fishing, eateries, or many other opportunities.

The closer to the water you travel, the more you will notice the scent of saltwater lingering in the air. This is especially true on humid days. Your hair is not your friend on those days; trust me! One of my favorite relaxing pastimes is to grab a coffee and park my truck on the sand. During one of the most difficult seasons of my life, my divorce, the sea was my refuge. I almost believed I needed to get away to find another place of healing, but it was there at the sea the whole entire time. I believe that if I had gone somewhere else in that season, I would have been avoiding my pain. The seaside was my space to quiet my soul, write out my frustrations, clear my head, and just be still.

What a funny little oxymoron that is, isn't it? I came to find stillness in a place that is anything but. The nature of the sea is not quiet; it's not still, and it certainly isn't restful. But that's the beauty of the sea. It encompasses both beauty and wild, the calm and the chaotic. Yet, it is balanced all the same. As I pen this chapter, the scent of salt lingers although it is not overpowering.

Sunkissed shells are scattered upon the shore; each one with its own story, I am sure. To my right, there is a partial remnant of what I've gathered was an old chimney. One would certainly think it is out of place here on the shoreline. It is miles away from its intended form. It is a broken, worn part chipped off even . . . stuck between two boulders unable to move. Why is it here? Was it ripped from the structure it was once a part of? Perhaps its removal was due to a renovation? Or what if it was by force? Did a hurricane decide to infiltrate the cement media and toss it about into the sea? How unexpected.

Upon closer examination, this piece of chimney appears to be quite old. The mortar looks as if it were from a time when things were purely handmade. Rustic in its demeanor with a bit of unevenness between the rows; the authenticity of the grout was truly unique. The bricks surely have seen better days, but the abrasiveness of the sea has refined the once sharp edges to some extent.

The Sea

Life is symmetrical to the sea. As we age and mature life has a way of refining us into who we were always meant to be. Sometimes, those waves crashing against us are fierce, yet most of the time we can withstand them. But oh, those other times . . . you know the ones I'm talking about. The times when it feels like the shore is becoming shorter in front of us, and the sky looks uncertain with unnerving impeding darkness. Yet, the sea also offers no comfort when the hurricane it births inches closer. At least this is how it seems. Tragic storms have the tendency to show us our true character. Good or bad. If we are wise, they allow us to see our weaknesses. We can then take the remnants of our own chimneys to see how we can either restore or renovate if necessary. We mustn't get angry at the storms, the sea, or ourselves when things crumble. When we fall on hard times or when we don't even have words to understand the "whys."

Hurricanes come and go as they please. They do not ask for your permission to swirl around a bit. They don't ask if this is a good time to pass over. They just come. Sometimes, they're strong enough to destroy everything in their path. In the summer of 2022, we had a few come into the Gulf and as each one inched closer, I was watchful to see which direction it would go. A person has to be prepared to make a decision about what they're going to do. Will they stay or pack up and get out of Dodge for a few days? I have horses, livestock, and my girls to think about. I can't just take this decision lightly or make it at the last minute. I must always have a plan in place to evacuate with livestock accommodations thought out.

In 2022 the hurricane that was headed straight for my region of Texas ended up not being very strong at all. We received heavy rain for a few hours, and that was the worst of it. My oldest said, "Mom was that it?" I replied, "Well I guess so, (with a laugh), let's go make some dinner."

Some years we haven't been so lucky. In the summer of 2017, my family experienced the destruction of Hurricane Harvey. Unless you have lived through such a storm you do not know what spine-chilling sounds spewing from these powerful sea monsters. The most beautiful sunsets precede them with deep oranges, reds and purples. Skies quickly turn strange colors with violent winds shortly after the sun seemingly ceases to exist. An eerie feeling lurks in the atmosphere until the last drop is poured from these storms.

Hurricane Harvy first hit my cousin's home in Rockport, Texas, and I kept having an awful feeling that we were next. We were told that it wouldn't hit my area, but I had an unnerving feeling that would not leave me be. Hours passed and as radar updates became harder to transmit, I caught a glimpse of this massive destructor coming straight toward us. There was no escaping it and no more time to pack up to run. The storm just had to be embraced.

I put my oldest to bed that night in my bed, so she would feel comfort and safety. Her sweet slumber gave me the peace I needed. Into the early morning hours, the wind started to gust, and trees rustled violently. I received screenshots of weather updates from everyone who was awake. Thankfully, we never lost power, but it did flicker constantly. I kept praying for my home to be spared, and I thought it was safe because we have a pier and beam foundation. As the hours passed, I anxiously looked outside to check the water levels—first the back window then the front porch and finally the garage. At that time, I drove a Ford Flex. I loved driving my vehicle, but I started to realize that it would be engulfed with water. I'd lose my vehicle. I ran back inside to check the level in the garage, and again I was disappointed. The water had risen and flooded my extra freezer, washer, and dryer.

That only meant one thing. The house was next. I went to a certain part of my home that was lower than the rest; yet for a third time, I was struck with disappointment. My home was taking on water at three o'clock in the morning. The water was eighteen inches above the ground outside.

One would have expected me to be in a state of panic, but I was rock-solid in believing that we were going to be more than fine. I knew that God was going to restore everything in the natural that was messed up. I couldn't explain it, but God had delivered me an unshakeable peace about that. Let me tell you when God restores, He makes it better than it was before.

Briskly, I moved around the house picking valuables up off the floor, and I put things up high just in case flooding got worse. The last thing in question remained unanswered: Where were we going to go? I called my sweet friend down the street who had a two-story home to see if we could wade the floodwaters to her house for refuge. She agreed, and I told her we'd be there as soon as we could. We couldn't drive, so the only option was to walk.

I packed important documents, chargers and a change of clothes in Ziploc bags, then put them in a trash bag inside a backpack. Next, I ran to the garage to grab our life jackets. The road was lower than the elevation of my home. There was no telling how deep the water was there. I opened the front door and told my daughter to hold on tight. We were about to walk down our driveway of roughly four car lengths. We would have to walk across another four properties down the street to my friend's home. Mind you, this was in the middle of Category-4 hurricane force wind and rain; lighting was flashing around us.

At that time, my daughter had just turned seven. As we walked down the street, we were unable to see the pavement which was covered in water by nearly two feet. The streetlights were all out of power. She held my hand tightly, and then I felt a pull on my arm. She had tripped and fallen into the water. I pulled her up quickly and with a barely audible sound, she said, "Mom I can't see It's too dark. How do we know we're not going to fall into the ditch?" I told her, "When the lighting flashes, look straight ahead and look for the light flashing on the two stop signs. We need to stay in the middle of those." So that's what we did. Flash by flash and step by step. What normally would have taken about five minutes to walk, took us nearly thirty minutes.

Finally, we reached my friend's home. We were safe. I knocked on the door, but there was no answer. We knocked again, and her husband came to the door. I'll tell you this next part because we can laugh about it now. With all the hurry and anxiety of the storm, she had forgotten to tell her husband about us coming over. He answered the door with his pistol, clearly a little startled. It was around four in the morning in the middle of a hurricane. We came inside, and we all had a good laugh; we can still laugh about that to this day.

How could something so simple as seawater be so destructive? Hurricane Harvey was about 280 miles wide; they called it the great 1,000-year flood.[5] According to the State of California Central Valley Flood Protection Board, the volume of rainfall from Hurricane Harvey could have filled the Great Salt Lake twice over![6] I was the worst flooding our country had ever endured. My property sustained so much water that my underground gas lines cracked from the weight. Our local weather station said that "nine trillion gallons of water fell from the storm [of] biblical proportions."

From its genesis, Hurricane Harvey lasted nearly a week. Though I can tell you it felt more like forever. What made it so detrimental was that it kept going out to the ocean, grabbing more water and dumping it back on land. Although Harvey didn't come close to the destruction of the 1900 storm that hit Galveston, Texas, recovery from Harvey's aftermath was a long process.

Hurricanes within us can be just as devastating as the storm we experienced that year. The nature of the sea often matches the nature of our hearts. There can be calm serenity or colossal winds whipping around rain bands of destruction. There can be an unsettled anxiousness about the unknown that the chaos causes us to feel. We tend to feel displaced when life's storms arise out of nowhere and move us from our secure safe places into the unknown.

After the storms pass, then comes the evaluation period in which we have to assess the damages and formulate a plan to repair or rebuild. When the insurance adjusters came out to evaluate damages after Hurricane Harvey, they left no detail unturned. They wanted to know how much of the water damage was storm-related versus how much was from spillage due to drivers on the road pushing water into my home. Then they looked at the structure. How were the foundation beams? How were the angles of the walls in comparison to the original blueprints? Then they looked at the windows, the doors, the roof, and the corner posts of all my external walls. Their goal was to determine what was good enough to stay and what had to be replaced. Then I had the daunting task of determining what items in the home were damaged enough to say that I had "lost" them. It was a headache to say the least.

My whole home was exposed to these evaluators in its most raw and delicate state. There was no hiding the stench of the floodwaters with air fresheners. There was no quick repair of the floors since they all had to be replaced. My whole home was in disarray and full of brokenness.

I can only imagine a tiny little piece of sea glass getting moved around a gigantic ocean during a hurricane. Did its origin begin in a place like Africa? How broken was it before it came to my shoreline? How many oceans or hurricanes did it have to cross? Or how many miles did it trek before the post-storm waves serenely delivered the tiny treasure to a redheaded woman writing her book amidst her own personal hurricane? I'll never know those answers, but if I could extract the stories, I imagine I'd have many tales to pen.

Despite what one might think, hurricanes do have some benefits. In the natural world, they help move sediments from the bays to the marshes to rejuvenate the precious nutrients for an ecosystem. Hurricane scientists report that hurricanes reduce coral reef temperatures, which in turn reduce thermal stresses. After Hurricane Harvey, I cannot tell you how many good things

I saw. I saw neighbors helping tear out each other's wet carpet. I saw my daughter's teacher come over to help dry out books and sort through toys. We saw friends pull out their smokers and cook whatever they could so people didn't have to worry about meals for their families. There are dozens of stories I could share, but I loved how my Lone Star State came together to support one another. Things eventually all got sorted out and restored.

Even during the post-hurricane processes, I still had peace. People asked me why I wasn't worried about everything, and my reply was always, "If God is who He says He is, He allowed this storm and knew it was coming. He also already knows what needs to be provided for it all to be fixed too." I had been through trials before, and I have also seen God pull through and fix things too. My foundation was solid because it was on Him.

If you don't have your feet firmly planted on the rock, you're going to drown in the sea. There is no way around it. In the Gospel of Matthew, Jesus tells us:

> *"Everyone then who hears these words of mine and does them will be like a wise man who built his house on the rock. And the rain fell, and the floods came, and the winds blew and beat on that house, but it did not fall, because it had been founded on the rock. And everyone who hears these words of mine and does not do them will be like a foolish man who built his house on the sand. And the rain fell, and the floods came, and the winds blew and beat against that house, and it fell, and great was the fall of it."*
>
> —Matthew 7:24–27 ESV

Even if you build your foundation one day at a time, remember Rome wasn't built in a day and neither were we. I certainly could have been overtaken with oceans of anxiety about how we were going to restore our home while still functioning with our day-to-day tasks. There was already a lot going on for our family with me working full time, my oldest playing soccer, being a scout troop manager, and my daughter being in school. Let me tell you God blessed us so much financially that He allowed our home to be one of the first ones to be repaired just in time for Thanksgiving. It wasn't apparent in the beginning of the hurricane damage why God expedited our home repairs. I found out I was pregnant with our rainbow baby. She was the joy after not only the physical storm that had passed but also after the storms of multiple painful miscarriages. In addition to this, our home became a warm inviting place for others to relax and feel refreshed while they were still going through their own repairs. God is good, and I am so thankful for His blessings during that season.

When you go where peace makes sense to you, you'll find it there. Sweet reader, no matter what kind of storms are formed from your oceans of hurt, the sea recedes, and the Son eventually warms your soul with peace and restoration once more.

Chapter 4 Journal Prompts

Eventually, the ocean has its own way of sorting everything out. Things that need to be washed ashore eventually do; they may take a while to do so. Do not rush your healing or let anyone else tell you that you should be farther along. This is your "sea" voyage. Take as much time as you need to with this chapter's prompts.

1. What was/is your ocean experience? In other words, to what depth does your "pain ocean" go?

2. What was/is your escape? Is it a healthy rest and healing, or does it feel uneasy or messy? Or is it even destructive behavior? (Please note I do not want you to self-shame here. You're being raw and vulnerable with yourself. It's OK to feel all the things. Just be honest with yourself here.)

3. How can you help to guard your heart against going to destructive habits when you feel like you want to escape the pain?

CHAPTER 5

Salt

The cure for anything is salt water – sweat, tears or the sea.
—Isak Dinesen

Oh, wonderful flavorful salt. It's one of those things you either love or you hate. Ironically, our body's calibration requires a certain amount of sodium to function. It has been discovered that the human body requires an estimated 500 mg of sodium daily.[7] Too little sodium and our bodies can go into shock. Too much and our blood pressure rises, our hearts enlarge, and other severe consequences may occur. Therefore, a perfect balance is required.

I am definitely not opposed to having French fries and ice cream combos. Besides, who could go without some good ole southern fried okra with a dash of salt on top. I should have re-thought the idea of writing this chapter sometime other than around bedtime; I most likely will be making a pantry run for a snack before too long. Food without the element of salt would be less than ideal; things taste better with it. The sensory receptors in our body recognize salt when it dissolves onto our palette. It is such an effective flavor enhancer; I believe that is why the Lord used it in His parables—to help us understand more easily. For example, in Matthew, He says, *"You are the salt of the earth. But if the salt loses its saltiness, how can it be made salty again? It is no longer good for anything, except to be thrown out and trampled underfoot"* (Matthew 5:13–16). When we accept Jesus into our hearts, we are like the flavor for the world to help preserve the kingdom values. We help keep the balance.

One of my dearest friends makes the most wonderful homemade ice cream. You are on her special list if you are invited to be her guest when she makes a batch of cookies and ice cream deliciousness. My sweet friend, I would trade your favorite chocolate bar for some ice cream.

When my friend explained the importance of salt in the creamery process, I was surprised because one would not think that salt would be such a key component in something is so sweet. But I learned that to turn the ingredients into the decadent treat, ice and salt are essential. Not just any kind of salt mind you, it needs to be rock salt. As the cream is being turned, this creates energy, and that energy is transferred to the ice. The salt doesn't keep the ice from melting; rather it lowers the temperature at which the water freezes, creating a slushy mix that is colder than ice. This brings the temperature of the ice cream down to a freezing point. Salt, in this case, helped to create something new.

In other instances, salt can be detrimental to the elements it engulfs. Growing up on the Gulf Coast, I have become well versed in the damage sodium-weighted air can cause. It seems every few years I have to sand or repaint some of my patio furniture or outside fixtures due to the accumulation of corrosion and rust. I do understand that this is a natural environmental breakdown process. I can choose to adapt to my surroundings, complain, or move. The choice is mine and mine alone.

The Bible story about Lot's wife resonates with me. Genesis 19:26 says, *"But Lot's wife looked back, and she became a pillar of salt."* It is so easy to look back on situations, experiences, or events and allow bitterness to seep in like poison. I'm no exception to this and have been there a time or two myself. I've had my share of relationships and friendships that ended poorly. I was not the nicest person in my thoughts or even my words and actions at times. I would think, "I can't believe they would ever dare say or do those things to me!" I would be unable to let the situations go; I was acting like Lot's wife. My heart was turning back and into a pillar of salt for the unforgiveness I was harboring. It's very easy to be consumed by such thoughts.

After going around the mountain of growth, the Holy Spirit gently whispered to me, telling me that I needed to learn true grace and forgiveness. My desire to not be destroyed like Lot's wife is much greater than my harbored emotions. Until we learn what God is requiring us to learn, we can't level up. I don't know about you, but I never want to have a forty-year desert experience just to learn a lesson like the Israelites had to. I'd much rather learn it the first time. Due to their stubbornness, most of them never entered the promise land; only a select few were allowed to.

Salt is also beneficial to replenish key elements for our bodies. As discussed previously in this chapter, our bodies require the element. Sodium is an electrolyte and can help your body maintain balance and blood volume. It helps your cells keep the right amount of fluid in them. When we sweat, we lose sodium quickly during perspiration; it is one of the first minerals to be expelled from our bodies. We can feel sluggish or irritable when we lose too much too fast. On the flip side, it really doesn't take much to replenish it. This is why you feel better after working out and drinking something like Pedialyte or Powerade.

We have horses at our house and the rule is we wash them after our ride or at the end of a hot summer day. The reason behind it, you might ask: Salt. My daughter's mare will begin to sweat at the beginning of daybreak when the sun is barely over the horizon. Within an hour of the sun being out, she is drenched in sweat. During the summer, she will sweat so much that when we wash her off, the salt turns foamy. We keep the water hose on her until it runs off clear. That's how we know we've rinsed her thoroughly. Any horse that is exercised heavily can sweat up to four gallons per hour!

When we ride for our performance practices, we will say that if there's no sweat, then we didn't work hard enough. A good horse and rider team are made from wet saddle pads. If we don't wash horses off, the salt will dry on their hair and skin resulting in hair loss in the coming days. Sometimes, the salt that comes off them is so thick it's like scraping butter off their backs. It's a tedious task to make sure they're thoroughly clean, but it's one that's worth it to sustain healthy horses. To maintain their mineral levels after vigorous exercise, we offer salt blocks or provide them with an electrolyte powder for replenishment. According to The Hay Pillow, an idle horse weighing 1,000 pounds needs a minimum of two tablespoons of salt a day. An active horse needs a little more than this.[8]

Monique Warren says that "salt is an inexpensive insurance policy." Salt is also a natural exfoliant. Yes, it burns when you pour it into an open wound; however, the point here is that salt acts as a cleanser. When it is scrubbed against dead skin, the debris falls away, and we feel rejuvenated. Our skin feels softer and smoother. If we pour granules of Epson salt into our bath water, it creates a healthy environment for our body to detox from the pollutants built up in our cells. According to Amin, a board-certified dermatologist, "Salt acts as a mechanical exfoliant and scrub, removing dead skin cells. Through osmotic actions, salts absorb toxins and draw out dirt and oil. Improved pore size is another benefit."[9]

Salt is necessary for ocean life to thrive; the National Oceanic and Atmospheric Administration (NOAA) has discovered that the salt in the ocean comes from land runoff or openings in the ocean floor. NOAA explains:

> Another source of salt in the ocean is hydrothermal fluids, which come from vents in the seafloor. Ocean water seeps into cracks in the seafloor and is heated by magma from the Earth's core. The heat causes a series of chemical reactions. The water tends to lose oxygen, magnesium, and sulfates, and pick up metals such as iron, zinc, and copper from surrounding rocks. The heated water is released through vents in the seafloor, carrying the metals with it. Some ocean salts come from underwater volcanic eruptions, which directly release minerals into the ocean.[10]

Sea life would not be able to survive without the ocean's salinity. Their precious lives depend on it. For example, fish have adapted to salt levels in the ocean; without its presence, they would lose the electrolyte balance essential for their bodies, and they would fail to function properly.[11]

Sea glass forms by having abrasive sea salt gradually scrub against the glass so that month by month, the glass is refined. It is not a quick process as the edges of the glass slowly erode giving the glass its frosted appearance. Otherwise, the glass would remain translucent and return to the shoreline broken as it was before. Sweet reader, sometimes life is going to deliver the sting to you—just like salt being poured into a wound. It will burn and feel uncomfortable for a time—perhaps even unbearable. Your parental heart may feel the pain of teenage hormones ripping your heart to shreds. You, friend heart, may feel the unkind words from someone who was once a very close friend. No matter the circumstance, abrasives come in many forms in different seasons.

In my twenties, I volunteered with an organization for many years. I started out as a troop coordinator, then became an assistant unit manager; before I knew it, I was elected as the area service unit manager. This meant that I was in charge of the entire organization for my city. I coordinated with our area leaders and transmitted information to my troop leaders. I was also responsible for monthly leader meetings. I had to keep my eyes on the leaders and the girls they were leaders for; I made sure special events were planned, delivered training, and approved budgets. My role also included marketing our organization to the community for recruitment, involvement, and support. It was certainly a lot of responsibility, and handling this at the age of twenty-two, well you can imagine this didn't go over well with some of the adults twice my age. I felt out of place at times because of my young age. Despite this, I knew that if God had put me in this position, then it was for a reason.

Sure, some of the leaders had more life experience; however, life had also given me circumstances that required me to feel and act much older than I was. As the program year advanced, I could feel the tensions growing with some of the older leaders. I was young, and I knew that. There came a time when we looked at the budget, and I saw how much we had been spending on a storage unit. We were also looking to cut costs somewhere, so I requested an inventory of the items. From that, I discovered that the storage unit contained all our camping and outdoor equipment. At the time, each troop was allowed to have their own gear, but our service unit had a set of equipment that could be used by any troop at any time free of charge. All they needed to do was check the items in and out with our outdoor coordinator.

I had a discussion with the coordinator and asked how often these items were used on an annual basis, what the upkeep was, and whether she had any ideas on where else we could store all our things. She got back with me with her records, and we found the usage was low. It was no longer justifiable to pay such high amounts of girl-earned funds to just storage. Our funds came from fundraisers the girls in our area did, so every penny needed to be stewarded intently. I brainstormed some ideas with her, and the best option we came up with was to have our equipment moved elsewhere.

We had talked with leaders from the next city over from us about where they store their items. They had a huge scout house with storage and extra room available at no cost for fellow scouts. It was a no-brainer to us that we should close our storage unit, move the items, and use those extra funds for the girls in our program.

At our next meeting, I proposed the idea and motioned for a vote to move our equipment. This went over well with everyone except a few people, one of which was an older woman who did not like me. My leadership was questioned in front of everyone, and I was told not only that I was too young but that I also was trying to change too many things. The vote to move the items passed, and this woman came to speak to me after the meeting had adjourned. She was not a happy camper (pun intended). She talked down to me and cussed me out; by the end of our talk, I felt very defeated. I spoke to my mother afterward about what happened as she had attended the meeting. I was just trying to do a good job and do what I thought was best for everyone; I wasn't trying to hurt anyone or make things worse.

My mother was also upset about what happened, but she offered me this Scripture: *"Don't let anyone look down on you because you are young, but set an example for the believers in speech, in conduct, in love, in faith and purity"* (1 Timothy 4:12). I didn't want to hear it, but it was something I needed. I didn't know this woman's walk with the Lord. I didn't know her personal struggles that surrounded her shortness toward me. I was just the person she felt she could unload her emotional hurts on. Her scapegoat and it wasn't fair.

However, after that conversation with my mom, I decided to soften my heart and have compassion for the woman who had confronted me. Just because I was young didn't mean I couldn't handle the position or that I had done anything wrong. I was changing things for the better and sometimes, people have a hard time accepting change. That was all. Her feelings weren't troublesome for me whatsoever.

My point is this. This woman was my sandpaper person—my salt abrasive, if you will. God knew that at twenty-two, I was going to need to grow, mature, and understand different people's opinions. Despite my softer nature, I needed to learn to not let criticism affect me personally. He saw the bigger picture back then, but I did not. He used that woman to bless me with an opportunity to show love and God's kindness to her. What I did not mention at the beginning of this story was that the year prior to this, I had started a new job. It was only the second job I had ever had. I was an office assistant and was very much on the bottom of the corporate ladder. It potential, and I loved the people I was working for.

The bigger picture God saw was that years down the road, He would position me to become the office manager and the boss when my boss was out of town. I was the one who would be responsible for sensitive information that was vested to only certain employees; I needed to keep that information classified and be trusted with it. I needed the skills God forged in my life at a younger age because again, I had people—employees, not scout leaders—for whom I would be in charge. I would face situations in which my patience would be tested; some employees sometimes require a stern hand. I also learned to offer a lot of grace to employees, sometimes knowing what they were feeling or struggling with in their personal lives. Time and time again, I have been told that in the corporate world, most of the job will be the people, not the work.

Had I not been prepared for these things at a younger age, I don't believe I would have had these opportunities afforded to me. God knew. God saw. God trusted. I am forever grateful for my boss, Barbara, who saw my potential at a younger age. She saw that I was moldable, adaptable, and teachable. These are all things we must be in the hands of the Potter.

Allow the refinement to wash over you as the sea kisses the edges of glass. God can handle all the details for you, your life and your circumstances, while this process is in motion. You must remember that it just takes time. Sea glass doesn't arrive overnight on the shore after one day of being tossed in the ocean. If it did, where would be the depth of authenticity? If He can take care of the birds and their needs, He can certainly take care of you that much more. If you're in an abrasive season, I promise you, things do get better. It may not be today, tomorrow, or even next year. Eventually though, the scrubbing will be complete, and you'll see the fruit from the hard-pressed season you endured.

Chapter 5 Journal Prompts

How does one refine broken edges? We sort through them and give ourselves an honest evaluation. This also requires us to give ourselves an honest opinion of where we are in the process of healing. Just like the salt refines the edges of sea glass, "salty situations" do the same for us.

1. What kinds of "abrasives" has God used or is using in your life for refinement? These could be in the form of a person, yourself, a situation, or an experience. (Perhaps it's a situation that made you pray more, or perhaps it's an accountability partner that prays with you. It could also be the consistent mentorship of someone during a trying season of life.)

2. How could these "abrasives" be used to refine you? (Here, you're taking what you listed above and figuring out an application process for them.)

3. Is there something that needs to be moved from your life which would allow replenishment? (For example, we know that Epsom salt baths help reduce inflammation and are used to detox our body so we can feel good. I had to take certain people out of my life because they were causing me to fall into some sinful habits. I needed to remove them so that I could allow God to heal my hurting heart and restore joy after my divorce.)

CHAPTER 6

Surfaces

Make your heart like a lake, with a calm, still surface and great depths of kindness.

—Laozi Tzu

Depending on where you're located, you may have many bodies of water available to see. Texas, where I live, offers abundant sunset-lit oceans, shimmering riverbeds, and serene lakes. I can travel to many of these if I choose to do so. Each body of water holds a similar refreshment for me; however, the design of each destination varies in its ecological design.

The sea can rage like a lion and birth storms of catastrophic capacity. There is an abundance of salt in the water and air which makes it cling heavily on your face during summer months. This offers beauty to the skin or destruction to structural things, just as we discussed in the previous chapter. Treasures found on the seashore are beautiful, but many have jagged surfaces that surround each one. The rocks are jagged from waves crashing into the shoreline with either graceful notes or strength from the Greek gods. The ocean's surface can change in an instant, and one must be prepared for every type of wave, circumstance, or storm imaginable.

The sea is too unpredictable to determine a percentage of a calm state. There are too many variables to consider and circumstances that could change in a matter of seconds. Before venturing off on a voyage, one must be mindful of erratic conditions, which may occur such as strong winds, swells, sudden storms, rip currents, and even rogue waves.

One of the most dangerous surfaces of the ocean resides in Drake Passage, Antarctica. It is infinitely unpredictable. I don't know about you, but it certainly is not on my travel bucket list. Voyagers have searched for the Drake Passage since the sixteenth century, which is named after the famous English explorer Sir Francis Drake. His ships sailed near the location but did not discover the actual passageway. They only discovered the waterways between the Atlantic and Pacific Oceans. According to the Rainforest website, "Drake passage has been known to be a ship graveyard for the number of wrecks it has caused over the centuries."[12]

Imagine being onboard a wooden vessel before modern times, getting tossed out of mid slumber only to find myself stumbling across the creaky wooden planks, somewhere between an awakened state and a dazed sleepy unconsciousness. I can see myself hoping and praying for the swells to settle and for winds to subside along with my pounding heart. I don't believe I would have voyaged often a few hundred years ago.

Jeff Bonaldi from The Explorers Passage, states that the passage is around 620 miles in width and on average has a depth of 11,150 feet. By way of comparison, he says, "The ocean floor is estimated at 15,700 feet deep around the southern and northern boundaries of the Passage." Travelers have also said the passageway has two surface states, aka the "Drake Lake" or the "Drake Shake."[13] Meaning, it either has a timid calm demeanor or swells as fierce as a Poseidon himself.

Our hearts are very much like this. We have peaceful seasons where the waves of our hearts are calm, serene, and still. Life feels easy and may feel seamlessly peaceful. Yet at other times, the surfaces of our hearts are like the "Drake Shake," rough from hurts and words we say to ourselves or that others have tossed onto us from their rough seas. The depth of some of those things can feel as deep as 15,000 feet with an ocean floor full of shipwrecked emotions.

Sailors live by an old saying: "Pink at night sailors delight, pink in the morning sailors warning." If one is caught in the midst of rough seas, one had better be prepared for any circumstances that could arise. Certain necessities might include boat repair supplies, first aid kit, clothes for weather conditions, food, drinks, a compass, an anchor and any other items a sailor might need for safe travels. Personally, chocolate and a life jacket would be essentials for me. But that's me.

Thankfully, sailing is a much easier lifestyle now versus hundreds of years ago. Conditions back then were cramped, and disease was rampant. Scurvy was the most common illness. Temperature regulation was scarce, and fire was usually only allowed in the kitchen. Heavy coats and wool blankets were a must if one was sailing in colder climates. These were certainly not ideal conditions to maintain a healthy lifestyle. Sea life was harsh.

Sometimes, the sea's surfaces can be incredibly calm. I've been at the water's edge to witness this myself. The water can be so calm that a serene peacefulness seemingly trances you into a slumber. The term *slack tide* refers to the short period when there is no movement either way in the tidal stream; this is known as the safest time for swimmers.[14] You can think of slack tide as the parallel to those peaceful waters or seasons in our life when we feel safe or peaceful for things to happen. Slack tide only happens shorty before or after high and low tide and typically lasts twenty to thirty minutes. For scuba divers and swimmers alike, it is the safest time to enjoy the water and relax. When our heart waters align with the peacefulness of the Lord, we feel slack from stresses in our life. Lindi Osborne from Swim Guide also says, "It is important to be aware of not only which tides will be best for your desired activity, but also how to avoid getting stranded or caught in one."[15] This is equally true for certain seasons in our life. If I am stressed to the max at work, worried about my children, and have an active extracurricular season, it is wise for me to avoid making big decisions during that time.

It would be equally wise for me to pose questions to myself such as, if I have to make a decision during this time, would it be rushed? Should I wait to make a move in a certain area until my heart and mind don't feel overwhelmed or heavy?

In the summer of 2022, my daughters and I went on vacation with my parents. We traveled a few hours north of our homes up to a lake that had a place for serenity and fishing. Most of the bodies of water near my home contain salt water. It was a nice change of pace to be able to enjoy the fresh water from the lake where the surface of a lake remains in a state of calmness. Instead of the water crashing against the shorelines, it grazes the shore with a wispy feather kiss. The sun glimmers on the water, highlighting the sedating peaks of the small waves. When one looks further out onto the lake's surface, it appears to be glassed over, and the waves merge into a smooth facade. It's almost as if there were no movement at all, drawing you into a tranquil peacefulness.

Despite these bodies of water being drastically different in composition, chemical makeup, and natural ascetics, there are similarities. The ocean is vast, so when ripples are cast, they aren't particularly noticeable, but they still exist. If the same action is cast upon a lake, it's much more noticeable. The lake surface doesn't move as much; it's calmer.

Depending on what season of life we're in, our hearts could match the sea or lake quite easily. It could even change day to day or month to month. We are ever growing, ever evolving, ever changing. Life gives us opportunities to grow and mature. When we fail to learn a lesson, we keep going around the mountain until we do.

Let me ask you this: what kind of ripples are you seeing on your heart's surface? Are they soft and delicate matching the motion in your soul? Are they ascending into parts of your life while nudging positive outcomes? Or are they larger, more frequent and constant? Are they nagging you with the idea of change you may not feel quite ready for yet? We'll dive into these questions when we move into the journal prompt section, but I wanted to plant the seeds for you to start to ponder on these ideas.

How sad it would be if the sea were ever 100 percent calm, still, and quiet. I was reminded by a dear friend of mine, that no matter the state of the surface, a calm state is relative if you consider the all the seas. Despite the waves feeling as though they're taunting us with a grave demeanor, perhaps it's OK if they are what they are. They are present alongside the rest of our emotions. They help gauge us alongside our basic levels of function.

I feel as if my heart is in a state like the ocean more often than not. There are calm moments as well; it's just that the motion is constant. Parts are calm and parts are not. The ocean is both. I am both. We are both. Calm yet constantly changing, moving, and evolving into the person we're growing into. I have had a few times when I'd go to write when the water was in the most beautiful glassy picturesque state. It was as if the far-off edge of the water had melted into the sunset, and they were one with each other—a perfect harmonious state.

In the fall of 2020, I went to the Seawall at Galveston Island to photograph the evening sky the day before a hurricane came in. (Trust me I didn't put myself in a dangerous predicament; it was all done safely.) The evening sky was lit up with gorgeous reds, oranges, and yellows. It gave the sky an incredible contrast against the deep midnight gray clouds rolling in. After photographing the sunset, I moved to a different area to gaze upon the ocean to see what the waves looked like.

Wind gusts were picking up as the waves crashed along the cement and wooden beams beneath the pier. My life at the time matched the state of the ocean. Per the Douglas Scale, everything was about a degree of eight before my eyes and in my heart. I was disappointed, frustrated, sad, and very overwhelmed with life that year. Life was chaotic and unsteady—just like the waves. Things were no longer beneath the surface; I felt broken with all the sharp edges cutting into me. How in the world was God going to smooth these edges out? How was I ever going to resemble a piece of sea glass?

After a little bit of time . . . actually, scratch that. After a lot of time, I could feel a change in my heart sprout. I could slowly feel the rough surfaces soften, but it took a lot of time. Any person who tells you that their healing from hurt was quick, overnight, or instant is not telling you the truth. Wounds that run as deep as a walnut tree, take a lot of patience, effort, grace, and time to heal.

I could sit by the sea for hours just to hear the waves crashing along the shoreline. I like to imagine that as the sea comes to me in all its powerful glory, it brings a renewed freshness to my soul. Then as the waves recede into its depths, the sea takes all the things weighing me down—all the hurt, the sorrow, the anxiousness, and frustrations. I sit there breathing the sea air into my lungs and breathing out the rest.

As our surfaces become more refined, it doesn't mean we don't have painful memories or current situations we're working through. All those pieces, healed or not, remain. In my thirty-plus years of living, there are experiences I have healed from and some I have not. It's all been a journey and a process. I'm still struggling to forgive some people for what was done years ago. Others, I have allowed God to overtake the experience from me, and forgiveness has blossomed effortlessly. Our rough surfaces become softer by the healing we allow to come.

We become mature in heart when we recognize and validate our varying degrees of "heart" waves. If we're reactive in our responses, we should consider whether there is something that we need to dig into deeper, something that is causing us to react that way. If we're feeling withdrawn and retract inward with our overall demeanor, are we feeling hurt by someone's words or actions? Are we feeling nervous, anxious, or fearful to speak up about how this is affecting us? Proverbs 4:23 says that we need to guard our hearts: *"Above all else, guard your heart, for everything you do flows from it."* This is vastly different from modern culture's view that you should "follow your heart." It is imperative that we learn how to check the degree of our hearts if we are to function in the healthiest way possible.

Sometimes, this means using a journal. It could also mean setting aside quiet time by ourselves to process emotions. If I'm going through a difficult season with someone, I do not want to be around them. I know I'll have at some point. For me, it's better if I have some alone time to process my feelings, so I don't act in an immature manner or say something that I'll regret. I need to let my internal pot simmer down. Another way I process things is sharing coffee with a trusted friend and talking things out—sometimes until two in the morning in my living room. My best friend and I have done this countless times, but I cannot tell you how much I have valued those times. They have been good for the soul.

When waves of hurt are colossal, like those that occur in hurricanes, the damage can affect not only us but others also. I researched sizes of waves for this chapter and discovered a wave gauge called the Douglas Sea Scale. My research from Jackon

Parton and an encyclopedia, uncovered this scale was created by the English Admiral H. P. Douglas in 1917.[16] The reason he created it was so that sailors could estimate their voyages for roughness. Were they going to be able to carry out their sail? If it was a navy ship, would they be able to complete their mission or reach enemy waters safely? Douglas's method consists of a few scales measuring the wave height and then the state of the swells otherwise known as the state of the sea.

The state of the sea starts off with no swells; it's calm and glassy. As the wind increases and the waves climb to biblical proportions, the state of the sea is classified as phenomenal, and height is indefinable. This information is comparable to our emotions and our state of well-being. I put a very basic feelings chart next to the Douglas Sea Scale. In doing so, it gave me a visual aid for my emotions or storms within my own heart. We'll use this more in the journal section but for now I just wanted to introduce the concept.

Douglas Sea Scale Degree	Wave Height (m)	Description of wave	Feelings
0	No wave	Calm (Glassy)	I am feeling great.
1	0 – .01	Calm (Rippled)	I am relaxed and happy.
2	.1 – .5	Smooth	I am cool and collected.
3	.5 – 1.25	Slight	I am OK.
4	1.25 – 2.5	Moderate	This is hard. but I'm in control.
5	2.5 – 4	Rough	I am getting uncomfortable.
6	4 – 6	Very Rough	I am heating up.
7	6 – 9	High	I am boiling.
8	9 – 14	Very High	I am ready to explode.
9	14 +	Phenomenal	I am out of control.

Emotions are like waves. They change, they move, they are not constant. One day they could be calm, and next day they could be like a rough sea with red flags posted from beach patrol. This doesn't mean we are crazy or that we need to think we're emotionally imbalanced. It just means we're human.

Even as a young child, my older daughter had big emotions. Sometimes, she'd get upset over things that might not have bothered others. Another parent once told me that my daughter was overly sensitive. It made my blood boil to have someone talk about my child like this. I had to walk away from the conversation because I wanted to harp on her for being so rude. However, I did not. Emotions are not bad, and we will sail into that a little more in the next chapter. I do believe that God gave emotions to us for a reason. Yes, my daughter had the propensity to feel things and feel them deeply. She is 100 percent her mother's child, and I admit I am the exact same way, but I see the bigger picture. A heart that feels deeply is going to be one that is sensitive to the Holy Spirit to see things how He sees them. Such a person will see the people around her who are hurting and need peace, comfort, and hope.

My youngest daughter is completely the opposite. God gave her a bold personality with sweet edges to round it out. Whatever her calling is, the world and her generation are going to need that kind of spice. I pray that God gives me the wisdom of how to not necessarily tame those waves in her, but to direct them for productive actions. I love what Ephesians says as a nice little reminder of how much He plans in advance for our children and even us: *"For we are God's handiwork, created in Christ Jesus to do good works, which God prepared in advance for us to do"* (Ephesians 2:10).

However high the wave of life you're treading, allow the Lord to hold the hurt with you. He'll sit with you. He'll be right there in the boat or even swim into the sea if that's where you are. You're not alone. Allow him to calm the waves, sort out the healing, and wash over you with warm peace that passes absolutely all understanding. When the waves are unsteady, He is not: *"You rule the swelling of the sea; when its waves rise, You still them"* (Psalm 89:9 NASB1995).

Chapter 6 Journal Prompts

1. We're going to be looking at the wave scale in comparison to emotions or an experience to see where you are with them. What are pieces of your heart that are struggling to find smoother surfaces? How do they make you feel? Think about some situations, either past or present, that were hard for you. This could range from anything about a relationship with people in your life, the relationship with yourself, or even an experience that has happened. (We'll dig more into emotions in Chapter 7, for now we're just listing things out and acknowledging them.)

Places of hurt/Situation	Emotion you're feeling with that?

2. Next let's look at the chart introduced earlier in this chapter. Evaluate which degree of "wave" you experience or are going through with each place of hurt. Some waves might be small whereas others might be larger. This is all OK. Go back to the list you created, and next each entry, write the corresponding degree. We are just using this as a gauge.

Douglas Sea Scale Degree	Wave Height (m)	Description of wave	Feelings
0	No wave	Calm (Glassy)	I am feeling great.
1	0 – .01	Calm (Rippled)	I am relaxed and happy.
2	.1 – .5	Smooth	I am cool and collected.
3	.5 – 1.25	Slight	I am OK.
4	1.25 – 2.5	Moderate	This is hard but, I'm in control.
5	2.5 – 4	Rough	I am getting uncomfortable.
6	4 – 6	Very Rough	I am heating up.
7	6 – 9	High	I am boiling.
8	9 – 14	Very High	I am ready to explode.
9	14 +	Phenomenal	I am out of control.

Example:

Degree	Places of hurt/Situation	Emotion you're feeling with that?
3	Divorce	Disappointed
7	Intimacy Trauma	Inadequate
5	Disagreement with my daughter	Anxious/Frustrated

Special Note from the Author: Now that you've evaluated everything, we're going to press pause. Some of these situations or places of hurt are painful. There is no quick fix or healing for them. If you need to stop here for a bit before moving onto the next part or even the next chapter, I just want to tell you, that's OK.

3. In this last prompt for Chapter 6, journal about what you think is a healthy way to start or continue to heal from this moment forward. You don't have to put these actions in place right now if you're not ready to. I encourage you to write some ideas that would be beneficial to you.

The healthiest way I found to heal was to journal and continue to see my counselor. She helped me work through what I was burying in my heart, what was unhealed from my childhood, and what I was grieving because of my divorce. That was what I needed to do for me.

Everyone's journey is different; please remember that and let no one, even yourself, take your testimony away. (At the end of Chapter 7, we'll be evaluating the emotional side of these places.)

CHAPTER 7

Tumbling About

When you pass through the waters, I will be with you.
—Isaiah 43:2 NKJV

As much as we don't like the breaking, we equally do not enjoy the uncomfortable season that follows. There is no going around them. Our choices are to embrace these seasons or complain about them. Both choices are hard, and I can't say that I've never complained because I certainly have. To embrace is to accept or support (a belief, theory or change) willingly and enthusiastically.

Objects of the sea do not get a choice when they are tumbling about amongst the waves or ocean floor. They simply exist or live with the circumstances the ocean provides. We have the capacity to host these ever-changing things that shape our day, our decisions, or our course of fate even. Life would be boring without our experiences, challenges, and circumstances.

However, my oh my, the waves I have ridden due to them. When situations arise, we can cognitively respond to accept whatever is at hand, or we can allow negative emotions to swell within us.

During my years of marriage counseling, I learned many things about myself. I am most definitely a strong, independent woman, largely because life presented me with circumstances that pushed me to maturity sooner than most my age. As I have shared previously, my mother fell ill when I was ten years old. I immediately assumed the role of being a caretaker while maintaining the role of being a big sister. I had a choice: I could embrace my circumstances or grumble. For the most part, I embraced the situation at hand. I can't say that was always though; when I look back, I see a little girl hurting on the inside who just wanted to be a normal child. I wanted to be taken care of too. The sting of that season still brings tears to my eyes even now twenty-eight years later.

This was a wounded place for me. It was uncomfortable to face, but I can see how it was necessary for my refinement. My counselor wanted me to do was dig deeper into my root emotions to heal those wounded areas. I learned that it's OK to think back on memories and tear up. However, if those recollections are causing you to shut down and shut off emotional responses, you're not healed yet. I know it's painful, and I know it . . . well . . . it sucks. But it is prudent to keep digging.

My counselor gave me an emotions chart and asked me to study it. I was to write down my thoughts about what I felt growing up the way I did. I couldn't help but think, "Are you serious? I have to color wheel my feelings?" I wanted to believe I was fine; I wanted to believe I didn't need to do this exercise. I did what she asked, but it took me a little while to complete the task. It wasn't because of any reluctancy or procrastination but rather I realized I wasn't really healed at all. Just like you turn a compost pile to ensure the nutrients are equally distributed and it is aerated properly, my emotions needed a turning. A tumble about if you will.

I was mad that I didn't feel like I had a childhood. I was mad that I didn't get to have a healthy mom like everyone else did. I was scared and anxious for years because every day we didn't know whether my mother was going to make it. There were countless times I was doing homework in a hospital waiting room. There were also countless times I had to call an ambulance to our home because she wasn't feeling all right. I was mad because I didn't want to be in that situation. I felt confused because I didn't know how to raise my younger brother. What proper instruction did I have or qualifications for the role of substitute parent?

The point is, I was a hurt little girl who didn't understand what was happening, but I felt like I didn't have a choice except to grow up. Over the course of several months in counseling, my top of the surface emotions was starting to break down to reveal their root causes. To clarify, let me explain a little further. Looking at the emotion wheel I had to work backward to discover the root of the emotion I was feeling on the surface. To do so, I looked at the emotion in the middle of the wheel, decided which emotion under the surface emotion was driving it and finally was able to trace everything back to the root of the emotion.

- On the surface I was feeling mad about my childhood.
    - » Under the surface I was hurt.
        - » The root was feeling jealous of my peers for having a normal childhood.

- On the surface I was feeling mad about having an unhealthy mother.
  - » Under the surface I was angry.
    - » The root was I was frustrated they couldn't fix her.

- On the surface I was scared about the future.
  - » Under the surface I was anxious.
    - » The root was I was embarrassed because I didn't know what to do.

- On the surface I was mad; I didn't want to be in this situation.
  - » Under the surface I was angry.
    - » The root was I was frustrated because I just wanted to have a normal family.

- On the surface I was scared about raising my brother.
  - » Under the surface I felt insecure.
    - » The root was I felt foolish for not knowing what to do, but how could I have known?

- On the surface I was sad about missing my dad when he had to work two jobs.
  - » Under the surface I was ashamed and lonely.
    - » The roots were (1) feeling stupid for feeling sad and (2) feeling inadequate for feeling like I should be doing more even though I was doing more than enough already.

It's not pretty, I know. It is quite messy, but it is my story. It was my tumbling and my refinement. God already knew the outcome even though I didn't. I have always believed that if God didn't want us to have emotions, he wouldn't have given them to us.

Emotions are not bad. They are our gauge to tell us where we are. It is when we get stuck in the pits of their ocean that destructive courses may arise. Even Jesus had emotions. The Bible tells us in John 11:35 that He wept for the death of his friend Lazarus. In Mark 11:15–18, the Scripture tells of His holy anger because His house had been turned into a place of business:

> *On reaching Jerusalem, Jesus entered the temple courts and began driving out those who were buying and selling there. He overturned the tables of the money changers and the benches of those selling doves, and would not allow anyone to carry merchandise through the temple courts. And as he taught them, he said, "Is it not written: 'My house will be called a house of prayer for all nations'? But you have made it 'a den of robbers.'" The chief priests and the teachers of the law heard this and began looking for a way to kill him, for they feared him, because the whole crowd was amazed at his teaching.*

As an exercise, my counselor wanted me to write a letter to my younger wounded self. Let me tell you I did not want to do that at all. All my excuses started to surface. I told myself that this exercise would solve zilch—that it was a waste of time. In reality though, I didn't want to do it because I was afraid:

- If I let that hurt little girl inside of me go, who am I?
- Am I going to be OK after doing this?

My counselor was so sweet and patient with me. I am convinced she was absolutely a saint. She knew what I needed, and I am very thankful for God putting her in my path. In this letter to my younger wounded self, I was to forgive myself. I washed ashore to this beautiful statement by Paul Boese and wrote it in my notes during my journaling time: "Forgiveness does not change the past, but it does enlarge the future." I absolutely loved it. I can't change the facts about my childhood any more than we can change when the moon rises. I can still hold the power inside myself to heal, so the exponential effects of healing make my quality of life more enriching for my daughters and me.

Before writing the letter, I journaled a list of things to forgive myself for. Some were for past things, and some were for current things:

- Overworking.
- High expectations of myself.
- To always get things right.
- Being too hard on myself.
- Feeling ashamed of my childhood.
- Not sticking up for myself.
- Not saying what I really mean to say and feeling shy.
- Not standing up for what I really want in life.
- Feeling like a pushover and not having strong boundaries.

From that list I fashioned a letter to myself:

Dear Younger Self,

First off, let me just say, that you're gonna be OK, but it's gonna take a little longer than you think. You're going to experience heartache like you never have before, and just when you think you can't handle anymore . . . well, hun, there will be more. Ignore the phrase that everyone says, "God won't give you more than you can handle." Girl, that is bologna, lol. God will certainly give you more and then a little more . . . because you we're not meant to bare burdens. That is God's job. His yoke is easy, and His burden is light. Heed those words, because you will learn that you do not have to hold the world on your shoulders. It is OK to say no if something is going to put a strain on you, your time, your family, and your sanity. You are going to find so much freedom in that alone. And even if you do overcommit, God can give you a way out to make your heart calm and balanced.

Younger me, I know that trust is an area that is hard for you. The circumstances of life haven't always been fair to you. Your mom got sick; you took on responsibilities that were not yours, and you grew up really fast. Trust that you will be taken care of and that someone will be there to hold you up when you need it. Your parents did the best they could with the emotional abilities they had.

Yes, your childhood happened; no, it wasn't ideal, but look at you now. Make peace with your broken pieces, and you'll be more than OK.

Your insecurities have been great and that has made your beautiful loving heart feel cold at times. But let me tell you, there are good wholesome people who are going to fill your life with love. The places in your heart that you thought couldn't be whole, will be. Trust me when I say, in time, your heart . . . it will be better than you thought. But it will take time. Stick up for things that are important to you; stand up for you and the voice you have inside. This is your truest self, and it is wonderful. Stand firm in who you were made to be.

You are a good, loving, wholesome person. Remember that God has held every tear even when you have felt alone this side of Heaven. Take care of yourself and don't rush through life "just because you have to." Enjoy it, savor it, embrace the moments that are going to come and fill your life with joy.

Finally, learn to forgive yourself. Just because things haven't worked out the way you expected them to, this doesn't mean that they won't. It just may be a different, perhaps a more beautifully connected life. Be patient with yourself and don't rush yourself "because you have to." It's OK if you haven't made every single decision wisely. Did Paul, David, or Moses? No. Lol. So, younger self, don't "over-expect" things from yourself. Just live and live well. Life will throw curve balls, and I know that you will try to make sure you always make the right decision. But let me tell you, it's OK to make mistakes, and it's OK to not get it right all the time. Learn to weed out what is important, what is needed vs what is wanted.

Allow yourself to rest well. I'm not talking about just thinking about rest. I'm talking about quieting your soul, listening to God's direction, and just sitting in rest for a while if that's what you need. I know this is hard for you to do, but it's OK. Take deep breaths . . . for as long as you need them, and then let's move forward to a better you. The world is going to try to make you break and always keep you busy, but remember you have little eyes looking up to you. God gifted them to you, for you to be their mom and teach them how to live wholly, healthily, and wisely.

You've got this, younger me, and God will always give you what you need when you need it.

—Your healing older self

The tumbling about is most certainly uncomfortable. When glass makes its way through all the elements of the sea, I can only imagine the travel stories it would tell if it could. To personify sea glass briefly, perhaps the tale would go something like this:

> The waters were cold when we all took the plunge. Flecks of light speckled across the ocean's water like fireworks in July on a summer night sky. It was beautiful. My silky surfaces allowed the water to glide over me swiftly. Fur-

ther and further, I plummeted to a soft pillowlike ocean floor. Full of silt and sand, it scratched me. It hurt. It was uncomfortable. My once glossy surface was brushed with blemishes from the unforgiving ocean floor.

A force within this dark place keeps pushing me away from my places of comfort. I can't quite seem to grasp the reasoning behind it, but it is infuriating to me. I heard whispers from the others that it is something called the current. It pushes us for long distances some days. I'm uncomfortable with the pace with which it forces me forward.

I notice that my once clean-cut sharp edges are becoming softer. How will I cut my way through life now, I've wondered. The ocean is salty. It is lined with microscopic particles of sodium, and I fear my frosted patina has become permanent.

There is a warm inviting glow up ahead that the current has propelled me toward. The increasing warmth against me feels like home. It feels peaceful. The shoreline is nearing, and I have to say the ocean has done me kindly. No, I am not new, yet in the same regard I am. The tumbling about has tempered me to become what the current whispered to me . . . no longer broken but a beautiful new creation.

I think sometimes God makes us aware of the simple things for us to see how they parallel our lives. That's what sea glass is for me. It is a parallel to my own experiences in life. I've tumbled around until I've reached this point in my life. Some areas of my life are refined, and some are not. There are parts of me that still have to make their journey through the ocean to be refined and that is perfectly all right. Remember you are worthy of healing, and you are worthy of a beautiful life, even if it takes some tumbles along the way.

Chapter 7 Journal Prompts

1. As stated earlier in this chapter, emotions are not a bad thing; we dug into them a little bit with Chapter 6. Emotions are a gauge to tell us where we are on our journey. We're going to consider the places of hurt and extend our journaling about them here. Take the list you created in the Chapter 6 prompts and list them out one by one; then write about them. Let your pen flow freely. For me, this is a good step; I write nonstop and don't let my pen come up until I have it all out on paper. Afterward, I finally started to feel some relief. Take your time and don't feel bad if you feel emotional. It's OK to be vulnerable with yourself.

   (Write your list below.)

2. Now that you have your list, try to find what the root emotion is for each item. Here are a few of my emotional examples:

> I'm feeling embarrassed, which triggers my anxiety, and my root emotion is scared.
> I'm feeling frustrated, which triggers my anger, and my root emotion is mad.
> If I'm feeling relaxed which causes me to be more thoughtful, my root emotion is peace.

I'm feeling: _____
Which triggers/causes me to be more: _____
Root Emotion is *(Circle one):* Sad, Mad, Scared, Peace, Empowered, Joy

I'm feeling: _____
Which triggers/causes me to be more: _____
Root Emotion is *(Circle one):* Sad, Mad, Scared, Peace, Empowered, Joy

I'm feeling: _____
Which triggers/causes me to be more: _____
Root Emotion is *(Circle one):* Sad, Mad, Scared, Peace, Empowered, Joy

I'm feeling: _____
Which triggers/causes me to be more: _____
Root Emotion is *(Circle one):* Sad, Mad, Scared, Peace, Empowered, Joy

I'm feeling: _____
Which triggers/causes me to be more: _____
Root Emotion is *(Circle one):* Sad, Mad, Scared, Peace, Empowered, Joy

I'm feeling: _____
Which triggers/causes me to be more:_____
Root Emotion is *(Circle one):* Sad, Mad, Scared, Peace, Empowered, Joy

I'm feeling: _____
Which triggers/causes me to be more:_____
Root Emotion is *(Circle one):* Sad, Mad, Scared, Peace, Empowered, Joy

3. Evaluate whether you need to write a letter to yourself. (Remember that if you feel you need to, give yourself grace and show yourself kindness. Every time I worked through things that were emotionally difficult, I did something nice for myself right afterward. For me, that meant getting my favorite iced coffee, going out to a nature spot to soak in the scenery, or taking a warm bath. This may be a hard journal prompt for you, especially if there is trauma behind it. Be patient with yourself; you've got this!)

The Sea Glass Soul

CHAPTER 8

The Rocks

If there is no struggle, there is no progress.
—Frederick Douglass

The rocks . . . such an uncomfortable place to be. Some may question why I have a chapter about rocks in a book about sea glass. Honestly, this wasn't a planned chapter whatsoever. I thought God had already given me all the chapters for this book by the spring of 2021. However, when prompted by the Lord, I have learned it is best to follow His instructions. After all, that is what faith is all about, correct? The Apostle Paul says in 2 Corinthians 5:7, *"For we walk by faith, not by sight"* (NKJV).

One December evening, well really all that week, I struggled with some personal battles—the kind of battles that come from being freshly divorced. Things were different, creaks sounded more daunting, and tasks seemed more difficult. I was in a state of grief. This season also consisted of learning how to be alone, accepting that some people will never change—no matter how much you want them too. The idea of being able to co-parent well seemed like a far-off goal and something that might never become a reality at all. In the end though, I missed my girls like crazy because they were at their dad's house for the weekend. Their sweet little cheeky faces weren't popping around the corner at me. Laughs from across the couch weren't echoing off the walls. There was nothing audible except the subtle ring of wind chimes, horse neighs, and the breath expelled from my lungs.

It had been the kind of week in which I had eaten more pasta and cookies and cried more than I'm going to admit on this parchment. I really wanted to hang out with some mom friends that week to take some of the fresh hurt of loneliness away just for a few hours. Unfortunately, my disappointment was exponentially increased as I read the texts coming over from my mom group. Everyone was too busy, sick, or had remembered their forgotten plans they needed to tend to. The activities I thought I was going to have were cancelled. I couldn't help but feel disappointed, resentful, angry, and jealous all at the same time.

I resented the sense of "normal" they were feeling and experiencing. It was holiday season after all, and it was supposed to feel joyful, full of the warm fuzzy feelings from the Christmas season. I was angry because I wanted my kids' company to help take the hurts away. However, that's such a heavy burden to place on their shoulders. Nor is that appropriate or fair. The divorce wasn't their fault nor was it in their life plans. Only Jesus could fill the hole of hurt that was festering. I was angry and jealous because I felt like I had been a nice person all my life and questioned the hand God had dealt me. Why was I still bearing the burden of doing all the hard things the other party didn't want to do? Being the responsible one? Where was my happy ending? Where were my happy holidays and Merry Christmas? I recognized later that it was not fair to toss my feelings onto my mom group. They had no idea how badly I wanted to engage with people other than my coworkers or myself. I felt like I needed fellowship with my crew. I was yearning for fellowship. I wanted an escape from the pain and hurt I was experiencing deep down in my soul.

Families were getting ready for holiday parties, enjoying their kids being silly making cookies and doing the "mom thing." Another sting that burned was we always held an annual Christmas light scavenger hunt. We always had a lot of fun putting these on. We'd gather at our home, send everyone out with a scavenger list and then the first person back won a prize and bragging rights for the year! I'd order pizza, make a big batch of homemade hot chocolate, eat cookies; we'd all have a good time until the midnight hour. My mama heart was grieving past memories and change.

It wasn't until late that cold December weekend that I realized God was trying to get my attention. He wanted me to get into His presence. He wanted some alone time with me. I needed to stop trying to distract myself by being busy or by hanging out with people just so I could numb hurts inside. He allowed all my plans to fall short just so I could learn the lesson of true intimacy with the Lord. During my time with Him, clear as day I recognized, I was amongst the rocks. I was washed ashore by grief waiting to be released—this kind of release isn't quick.

This requires the tools of our expert navigator. It takes intention. It takes feeling all your feelings and offering yourself compassion. Brené Brown says it best: "We run from grief because loss scares us, yet our hearts reach toward grief because the broken parts want to mend."[17] We aren't made to stay there. Some may think of being amongst the rocks as a season of being stuck. If you've been there for a while, you may even feel hopeless. But being wedged between rocks is just as important as any other season. Without it, our refinement would not be complete.

The epigraph I chose to begin this chapter with comes from a man who knew struggle well. In 1857 Frederick Douglass gave what is called the West India Emancipation Speech in New York as a precursor to the imminent Civil War.[18] He was a part of the anti-slavery movement and spoke courageously about his experiences as a slave. It well documented that slaves did not have the same rights as other Americans were afforded. Depending on their location and who their owners were, they weren't allowed to have any kind of literacy; they were stuck and oppressed. In fact, in 1831 it became illegal for slaves to be taught reading or writing.

When Douglass was a boy, God put him under the care of Mrs. Auld who was his owner's wife.[19] She worked hard to teach him how to read and write alongside her own son. Unfortunate circumstances would unfold from her husband's disapproval of this, and the teachings ceased. But Douglass would continue to learn things along the way as he grew into a young man. He taught his skills to other slaves. When his owner learned that Douglass was being educated, he was displeased and eventually sold him to a very cruel man who tried bridle Douglass's spirit. But he did not succeed. God showed favor to Douglass and made a way for him to escape to the North for freedom. He was removed from his rocky situation and set in high places to become one of the greatest encouragers of his time. As he aged, Douglass continued speaking out to correct the injustices against freed slaves and to offer much-needed truths, which helped pave the way for racial equality.[20]

Hear this: When God allows movement for you to be released from your rocks, He will not just let you go back to the same ocean that held you captive. He is going to expedite those waves to swiftly take you into your next season because that's where you are needed. Your rocky experience is going to be a testimony to someone else when they are in theirs. You're going to be picked up and held in positions you never dreamed of because when that light is shed on you, your value is going to be reflective and attractive to the people who need to see it.

Every time I come go out to the sea to write, God allows my eye to catch the matte finish of a piece of sea glass. I'll pick the pieces up to take home and put them in the collection jar my daughters and I started years ago. We must have hundreds of pieces now. You never know what you're going to find out there.

Once when I went to write, I had a stronger than usual desire to find some of my little treasures. To my dismay, what did I find? Nothing. Absolutely nothing. Naturally the human response in my head was like "Really God?! I'm coming out here to write about sea glass, not rocks! Where are the glass pieces?" You can guess God's response, right? There was no audible answer from Him or giant arrows from the heavens telling me where to find sea glass that day. So, I said, "Fine . . . but I'm here, writing the book you wanted me to do." As you can tell, I was a bit frustrated.

I can only imagine God's reaction to my moody temper tantrum. I admit, I was acting like a two-year-old. He was probably thinking, "All right, Jamie, go do what you think you're going to do. Then go ahead and get upset with me. I'm a big God, I can take it. I can't give you what you want right off the bat because you won't appreciate it as much if I did."

After my "gentle" reminder that I may not always find what I want on my time, I was sensing that God had a different plan in mind. This is usually the case I have found for many paths and designs for my life. For the most part after my divorce, I've been all right—not great, amazing, perfect, or worry-free. More like just in a state of all right. It has been a journey to say the least. Every season up until that point has been a part of the process to get me to sit on top of the rocks.

The sea of life had to take me far beyond my comfort zone. I believe it was to remove me from my bay of circumstances, which were unhealthy and toxic. It was to sail me away from my distractions because they weren't in line with my divinely written purpose. It was to allow those storms that also form in the sea to cleanse and wash over my soul. The sea salt had to neutralize my trauma so that I could see that the experiences were not my identity. It all had to be present to refine and taper my edges.

My writing place has a rocky shoreline a few miles out before the actual sandy beach begins. It consists of large boulders, shell, crushed rock, and sand. Birds are perched here and there. The occasional hermit crab pokes its tiny head above ground. Crevices are plentiful where things could be lost or found. Nature always finds a way to sprout new life in the empty spaces between the boulders. Whether it is a blade of grass, sunflower, or Texas sage . . . there is growth. Native horticulture finds a way to always be. Perhaps that's a lesson in and of itself. We have to allow natural growth to occur. It cannot be forced. What quality of fruit would be grown then?

Various items get washed ashore but who knows how long they stay there with salty air blowing across them, torrential rains packing them into place even more so than before. Not to mention that the scorching sun beats down dulling their color and changes the textures. Sometimes, notions get lodged in between multiple rocks making it nearly impossible for them to become free.

I nearly forgot to mention the darkness which can accumulate. I struggle with this because it is far too easy to let my mind be overcome with anxiety. I get overwhelmed with the "what-ifs" and the "God reallys." It's the place where the creepy crawlies like to visit. Symbolically, it's where we hear the lies from the enemy that say:

- You're not worthy of better places.
- You'll never find peace
- Love is not for you.
- This is as good as it gets.
- You're forgotten.
- No one cares.

Or what about the lies we tell ourselves:
- This is just who I am.
- My trauma made me act that way.
- I deserved this.
- I did something wrong, so I'm being punished.
- This person loves me, so the hurtful words or actions have to be OK with me.

The atmosphere and natural elements are never the same by the sea. The fragments I saw once before are no longer present. At some point something happened to create space, to create movement and to create an opportunity for them to be dislodged. They made their way elsewhere. Perhaps they're back in the ocean. Maybe someone else noticed the rocks or other pieces of sea glass and took them home.

Being amongst the rocks is only a season, and I am eternally thankful for knowing seasons do not last. This is why I love that God made different ones to help us understand the beauty in each of them. Perhaps there is purpose found in the rocky places. What if perseverance is being built during whatever season you're in right now because God knows you'll need to lean into that strength later? What if a testimony is being created because someone will need to hear your story just the way it was written to see freedom in their story? Finally, what if there is an appreciation that comes after this season? It will be sweet and satisfying like nectar to a hummingbird on an early summer day. Your blessings that follow may even come as a surprise to everyone including yourself. I know I've seen some in my life many times over!

During my frustrating day by the sea, the clouds began to swell and grow dark with fury. The wind rippled off the waves, birds fluttered away for shelter, and it began to rain. I was still disappointed that I had come all the way out to write but still hadn't seen any sea glass. Regrettably, it appeared that my time had forcibly come to an end. I quickly gathered my writing journal, coffee, and walked briskly to my truck. Looking down to keep the mist out of my eyes. Lo and behold, there was a small, frosted piece of sea glass resting amongst the rocks. It was in plain sight too. God hadn't forgotten. He just needed me to wait to find it, so I'd appreciate my little treasure that much more.

When I got in my truck, I placed it on top of my chapter journal for a little while with such admiration and tearful joy. I had no other plans that day but to focus on what the Lord wanted me to press into. I certainly poured out warm heavy tears as I wept in repentance for thinking God had forgotten me that day. I knew deep down that the Lord always has everything under control for me. But to physically see the confirmation of it and experience His faithfulness is entirely different. The waves of tears were getting me unstuck from my rocky places. I could feel the space being created for healing in my heart. There was allowance for the Lord to move where He needed to and for my brokenness to be dislodged.

Your healing is coming too, sweet reader. When those waves wash over you, you're going to feel the warmth of the water flood your soul, and it will offer the comfort you've been longing for.

Chapter 8 Journal Prompts

I have found that on the path to healing, tests and trials come up. God allows some of them to be present to act as a gauge. Maybe there was a situation we handled great and then the next situation we handled poorly.

The Rocks

1. What kind of "rocks" are you landing on?

2. Are you being consistent in the areas of your life you are working on?

3. Are you able to pass over these "rocks" to your shoreline goals? Are you getting hung up on jagged boulders and feel stuck in the crevices trying to break free one tide at a time?

CHAPTER 9

Tossed Back and Tempered by the Sea

You are allowed to be both a masterpiece and a work in progress.

—Sophia Bush

I have come to believe that as long as I come out to the sea to write, God will allow my eye to catch the treasured matte finish glimmer. This evening, I decided to treasure hunt before putting my pen to paper. I found six pieces of sea glass and tossed about that many back into the water. They weren't ready yet. The edges were not softened, and the patina not yet complete, so they needed to be returned to the sea for further tempering.

I wasn't quite sure what chapter I was coming out to write tonight. It was either going to be a session of simply jotting down my thoughts, or it would be a quiet time to get this chapter started. Either way, things were going to be accomplished. Things were going to move forward, and I had full faith God was going to meet me there. Faith is the complete trust or confidence in someone or something. I had removed my expectations of Him; I just wanted to be in His presence. The Lord isn't a genie for me to wish upon. I have a reverence for Him, knowing He will never put conditions on me. There wasn't going to be any, "Hey Jamie, maybe I'll show up or maybe I won't. I'm not sure yet." I know that He is faithful to show up every single time I need Him to.

This day was also the last day of the year. I enjoy looking back over the year and reflecting. I'll ask myself things like this: Am I still in the same place as I was mentally, spiritually, or physically this time last year? Did I grow, and if so, what methods worked well for that growth? What do I need to continue to work on? In my anxiousness of the new year coming, I woke up about in the early morning hours and could not for the life of me doze back off. I shared this with a friend, and she has shared the same experience. There is something to God waking us up often in the middle of the night. He knows how to get our attention in our most raw state.

As I began this chapter, I had been struggling with anxiety—more to the point, I was feeling like I was in a battle for my soul, mind, and at times my clarity. I was questioning many things—so much so that my blood pressure was on the rise. I had many questions about the future: What's going to happen next year?

Why aren't certain things moving yet? Did I hear God wrong? Is what I'm putting my effort into wishful thinking, or am I chasing an unreachable dream? Is this truly my purpose? What else can I do to help my children process the divorce? Is everything going to be all right? Lord, just tell me when to expect the bottom to fall out again. My heart was a jumbled mess.

Every year I also ask God for one word for the upcoming year, but I hadn't heard one yet. Earlier that day I was thinking that it was late afternoon, and I still heard nothing. What's the deal, Lord? And yes, clearly by now you may have noticed I've got some trust issues with my questions to Him all the time. Rest assured He and I are working on that. That's a mountain I'm still going around. Clear as day when I was putting away Christmas decorations, I had my word!

> Live.
> It wasn't live *and*, or live *but*, or live *also*.
> Just live.
> Don't worry about the details.
> Don't be anxious about how it's all going to come together.

Do not put any limits on what God can do and remember what He says in Philippians 4:6–7:

> *Do not be anxious about anything, but in every situation, by prayer and petition, with thanksgiving, present your requests to God. And the peace of God, which transcends all understanding, will guard your hearts and your minds in Christ Jesus.*

Every time I want to pick up the pieces and try to hurry the process, it is best to toss the pieces back. The year after my divorce was nothing but tossing things back. Tossing outdated versions of myself. Tossing out old memories—clearing out space in my home, my garage, my head, and ultimately my heart. It was not an overnight process either. I have had to take entire weekends to purge the physical items in my home. Sometimes, when I first started purge, I would have ten bags of trash sitting on my porch in addition to having both of my trash cans full to their brims. It was an excruciatingly painful process to sort through memories and tangible items that didn't serve a purpose anymore. What do you do with things that hold painful memories? What do you do with things that even the other party doesn't want but you feel stuck with?

There were books, DVDs, CDs, sheets, the marriage bed, odd and ends, and outdoor equipment that I had no use for. It felt overwhelming to keep storing all these items. I wanted peace. I wanted a clean space, but that meant cleaning up, and it meant doing it all alone. I didn't want my children to help with this because it wasn't like they asked for their parents to get divorced. They were the innocents in the mess. It wasn't their burden to bear whatsoever. Even though I was physically tossing things out, the most excruciating and important work wasn't the tangible things. It was the things in my heart that needed to be tossed out.

Looking inward and "spring cleaning" my heart wasn't exactly a walk in the park. I can look back over the past year and a half and see how much I've changed, grown, and matured. There was also some regressing, biting my tongue and groaning at the amount of grace I had to keep dishing out. I had many conversations with the Lord that went something like this, "Ya ummm God . . . I'm not ready to let that go yet. That's going in the keep pile." I had placed painful memories, unforgiveness, beginning of bitterness, and certain friendships in the back of my heart closet. I didn't want to make the hard decisions anymore; I was tired of making them.

There were so many pieces of myself that were still lodged amongst the rocks with sharp edges. If I could personify my heart, it would have said, "If I allow you to move these things, Lord, will it cut into another part of my heart? Will I begin to hemorrhage? Are you really going to fix it?" As my trust in Him increased, that's when the Lord picked up the pieces of my heart and tossed them back into the ocean for me. I wasn't strong enough at times to do so myself. I can see now that He allowed me to struggle to refine me just like sea glass that I had to be tossed back so I could be tempered by the seas of life circumstances.

To be tempered means to be strengthened. If God who loves us so much would send His only Son to come die on a cross for us, then He is going to take the time and allow situations to temper us into the best versions of ourselves. This is not only for our betterment, but also for those who are in our lives.

I wouldn't have believed the blessings that were coming to me even if God himself had told me face to face in person. I can only imagine God looking at me thinking, "If you only knew the things that would be coming later in 2022. There are people, places, positions, and relationships that I have prepared before you even asked me for them." I have found a lot of comfort in Psalm 139:5 to calm those anxious thoughts of mine: "

> *You go before me and follow me; you place your hand of blessing on my head"* (NLT).

Whenever my daughters and I find pieces of sea glass that do not have the completed patina, we gather our half-tempered pieces and throw them back in together. They just need a little more ocean time. My youngest loves this because she's a softball player and enjoys seeing how far she can throw them.

I have lived a good portion of my life under brokenness, disappointment, and hurt. Those moments, years, and relationships left scars that had deep roots. I dare say they are much like the shepherd's trees from the Kalahari Desert. Their root systems can reach about 230 feet down into the earth.[21] That's how deep some of those hurt places ran for me. The shepherd's trees thrive in the scorching temperature of the African terrain. Despite the heat beating down on its sturdy trunk, the tree still manages to thrive and bring life to its branches.

From my research on this beautiful tree, I learned that the local cultures are incredibly protective over shepherd's trees because of their ability to provide many benefits to people and animals in such dry and hot conditions. Different foods such as soup, coffee substitute, and edible berries can be made from various parts of the tree. Of course, due to their giving spirit, these trees are vulnerable to overuse or being destroyed.

Roots can be both good and bad. If they're the kind we don't want to toss out, those roots of bitterness, unforgiveness, or even unhealed anger will grow so deep that they will reach the core of who we are. Once they do, it is very difficult to remove them, or it takes a very long time to detangle. Sometimes, the only remedy is to chop some of the roots off. Root pruning can be painful but is most beneficial for longevity. The stress a tree undergoes when this is done is immense. There's no denying that. A study was done with trees that were left with decaying roots; the tree ended up weaker and eventually died. I've seen this happen in my own back yard more than once.

My lawn maintenance team were doing their weekly routine grass cutting just after a three-day rain span. The technician called to say that one of my trees was the victim of root rot and was about a foot from leaning onto my horse fence. This was not a small tree. It spanned roughly twenty feet in the air, so I knew the only solution was to have it cut down. I sent the payment and had them chop it down. I knew haste would make waste of my time, and I would have to repair a fence if I didn't act quickly. About six months later, my favorite tree in the back garden fell victim to the same root rot. Its system had weakened beneath it and could no longer sustain the weight from above. If I had seen those trees when they were saplings, perhaps they could have been saved but perhaps not. Either way, it runs parallel to the things our hearts hold within.

There's an old castle in my hometown, which was vacant for many years. It has recently been purchased and is in the process of being remodeled. I don't know exactly how long it had been without residents, but one can see from the road how overgrown it became. It wasn't until the new owners started the renovations that everyone knew how badly this town icon had deteriorated. Trellises of vines, roots, and natural elements had taken over the cold stone exterior. Stems of growth lurked over the arches, spreading their ever-growing grip to invade the cavity of what was once a beautiful home. Once removed, the roots left deep impressions showing where they thrived before being cut by landscaping blades. It would have been a silly notion for the new owners to leave the castle just as it was and set new shrubs and trees in the midst of it all. New plantings would have gotten choked out by toxic overgrowth soon after.

My mind is drawn back to the beauty and strength of the shepherd's tree, which survives because its roots run deep, anchoring it to the earth. When large animals come to forage or storms come to flood the plains, the tree is not moved by them. There was a reason God says in Deuteronomy 11:18 that we are to hide His words in our hearts: *"Fix these words of mine in your hearts and minds; tie them as symbols on your hands and bind them on your foreheads."* Every time that we do, another good root grows and anchors us closer to the core of who God made us to be. In his likeness. In his image. But we have to toss the old roots out first:

> *Then God said, "Let us make mankind in our image, in our likeness, so that they may rule over the fish in the sea and the birds in the sky, over the livestock and all the wild animals, and over all the creatures that move along the ground." So God created mankind in his own image, in the image of God he created them; male and female he created them.*
> —Genesis 1:26–27

It seems when God allows situations or circumstances to come into our lives that are meant to temper us, we do not like it. I went through a season with my oldest teenage daughter when I didn't know what was going to happen. I couldn't gauge her anymore; I didn't know what she was thinking and the only thing that pulled me through that dark season with her was faith and prayer. It was all I had, but it was enough. God knew I needed to strengthen my prayer life and my faith, so He allowed this season to come and do just that. I also needed to stop letting people use the phrase, "You need to do this" or "You should have done this." Those phrases weighed on me heavily more than they'll ever know. It had an engulfment upon my mind, which made me feel inadequate. It made me question what I thought was right—what I thought God was instructing me to do. Eventually, I recognized I was feeling shame through those phrases, and I corrected my thinking.

I can't even tell you how many tears I wept over that girl. I would drive home, crumble to my living room carpet and weep. There is a big difference between shedding a few tears and weeping with immense heartbreak over your child. I am so thankful for the people in my life who held me up like Aaron and Hur did for Moses. I was very weary from the spiritual battles that did not seem to end. The need for my inner circle to pray with me over things was great, but our God was greater. He did it. He healed it. He refined her and me. I certainly understand the meaning of fervent prayer now. Had it not been for those very rocky seas, I don't know if I truly would have learned that skill—one that I'm sure will be used many times for other things. A very close friend is a prayer warrior like no other. This woman has been fighting in the trenches with me, and I am eternally thankful for her dedication to intercede on my behalf. (She's also a fellow redhead, so we get along very well anyway.) She shared with me the following Scriptures during those dark times:

> *Confess your sins to each other and pray for each other so that you may be healed. The earnest prayer of a righteous person has great power and produces wonderful results.*
>
> —James 5:16 NLT

> *Rejoice always, pray without ceasing, in everything give thanks; for this is the will of God in Christ Jesus for you.*
>
> —1 Thessalonians 5:16–18 NKJV

It is hard to praise when your Jericho walls are high and it feels inevitable that they will crumble. It's even hard to pray when you feel like you have nothing left to mutter and the strength you have remaining is depleted. But that is where God shows up and shows off. Jesus carries us when we have nothing left, and the Holy Spirit speaks on our behalf.

There are parts of me that I can absolutely say are tempered well and look like the beautiful pieces of sea glass we have in our jar at home. But oh, those other pieces of me. They still have rough edges that need refining. It may only take one more sweep of a wave to soften, although they may need more. It may take several expeditions to be tossed back and tempered by the sea. Until then, we hold onto our faith and trust in the Lord's timing.

Chapter 9 Journal Prompts

Consistency will help us to "anneal." In other words, consistency helps us to slowly refine our broken edges. When heat is applied in the annealing process, the glass or metal piece must be cooled down slowly. Otherwise, the glass or metal will crack or break. If we rush our healing, we run the risk of cracking.

I can always gauge whether I have rushed myself through healing from a situation by my reactions to people or situations. If I have rushed the process, I tend to be on edge in my attitude, I may be a little feistier in my responses to others, or I may make decisions that are not true to myself.

Much like the annealing process, I have to allow the healing cycle to be completed. Annealing removes internal stresses and makes the piece tougher.

Consistent healing may look different for everyone but should include the same essential elements. Some examples of these include (but are not limited to) working on being our best selves, inner heart work, getting out the junk and replacing it with positive thoughts, cutting out toxic people or the toxic part of ourselves, checking ourselves against God's word, spending time in prayer and having reflection time.

1. In what ways do you believe you have been "tempered"? In other words, in what ways do you feel stronger or healed? (We will go into more detail about this in the next chapter's prompts, so for now just list them out.)

2. Are there any things you still need to "toss back"?

CHAPTER 10

Frosted Patina

From every wound there is a scar, and every scar tells a story. A story that says, "I survived."

—Craig Scott

Sea glass travels such a long way before it is adorned with its frosted patina. Beginning as a shattered piece of glass, fighting its way through the ocean to be sifted against the elements of refinement. This age-old progression is a natural chemical process and has stood the test of time for centuries. In the earlier chapters, we have looked at the individual steps a piece of glass has taken up until this point. We started with the very basic and raw materials a master crafter uses to mold a beautiful carafe, which are made as holding vessels for things we love to consume. I love my carafe to hold freshly squeezed lemonade.

We then voyaged through the broken pieces, the seas of life, and considered how salt functions as an abrasive that smooths out the broken edges and helps to reform sea glass. These were the middle stages of the voyage. I believe that the most important parts of my journey were the middle—the parts that were hard. Without looking at my surfaces and allowing God to tumble and find me, I would be stuck there. I gather that we all would remain stuck in the middle stages if we allowed ourselves to be.

Finally, we looked at why sea glass is sometimes tossed back into the sea and why we get tossed back into certain seasons. It isn't because God is mad at us or wishes to extend our pain. He is not a cruel heavenly father. We just need to be tempered by the seas of life a little longer.

The patina process does not happen overnight; rather it is quite a lengthy process. To break this stage down scientifically, patina is formed through a chemical progression of natural dehydration. Believe it or not, it can take around twenty-five years or more for one piece of glass to become completely frosted. This is solely dependent upon the pH levels of the body of water in which it resides; that is what determines the final characteristics of the piece.

According to Kristin Hissong at CoastalReview.org, the pH levels are high in the Atlantic Ocean and Great Lakes.[22] Most lakes will not yield frosted pieces due to their low salinity and pH levels. Glass is comprised of the following elements: silica, soda, lime, and a few other raw materials. Soda-lime glass is the most common form of glass available due to its chemical stability and inexpensive production costs. It becomes frosted when soda and lime dissolve in seawater, leaving small holes on the surface to be gently scrubbed by the ocean and softened. There would be no treasured beauties for us to find had the soda and lime not dissolved and washed away.

In like manner, some of the things within us that we think need to stay, need to dissolve. That is the only way for us to become smooth. Then and only then can the tiny holes left behind be filled with the Holy Spirit and the beauty of transformation. Our "pH" could be defined as all the elements of a season of life that presses us. Being an avid gardener, I know that pH levels of the soil are very important. The pH level of soil can range from zero to fourteen with a pH of 0 being more acidic and a pH of 7 being neutral. Anything above a neutral pH is a more alkaline state.[23] Sometimes, the pH that surrounds us is going to be intense and extreme, causing us to feel acidic in nature or heavy in our spirit. Our external experiences push us to exponential growth, and a lot of growing pains go along with it. In life, there are short seasons of "neutral-ness," in which there might be some very minor things that help us grow, but they aren't extreme. Perhaps it's as minor as taking a negative thought and turning it around to a positive one. Then there are alkaline seasons. These are the seasons of life that feel grueling and may even have us feeling scattered, uncertain, or depleted. I think the seasons when we feel most alone are the ones the Lord allows so that we get more in touch with Him.

Every time my character or parts of me have been refined, it was during seasons of uncomfortableness. It takes consistency, trials, mess-ups, lots of experience, and willingness to push through these seasons. Thankfully, the Lord delivers His genuine grace while we're growing. Grace is a gift of favor, mercy, and kindness; it's not something we deserve or earn by any merit.

My most memorable times in high school were when I was in the marching band. I went to a small-town USA high school where band was life! We were the "Pride of the Tribe." We went to our state's marching band competition every year and let me tell you, our band directors made us work for it. They knew the result came only from perseverance and discipline. We were pushed to persevere through the challenges because they knew the potential we had.

As a freshman, I went to summer band camp thinking, "Oh, how hard could this really be? We're just walking around on a football field playing our instruments." Let me tell you, Texas summers do not compare to other states in July or August. We had to be at school early in the morning because by noon, the temperature would be 100 degrees with 100 percent humidity, and it was 114 degrees in the shade. It was grueling, sweaty, and miserable. Echoes of our section leaders still linger in my head as they taught us to roll our feet and make it a HABIT. Which meant every time we heard, "Make it a HABIT," we were to think about rolling our feet from heel, arch, ball, and toe. Day after day, week after week of rolling our feet, our freshman class learned the marching band fundamentals. Our practice sessions were also complete with pit-stained T-shirts and daily charley horses in our calf muscles.

Toward the end of summer band camp, we would then join the rest of the members to learn the "show." This was not for the faint of heart either. Mind you it was still over 100 degrees.

We had to have something of substantial quality for the field no later than the first football game. Our directors were keen on us not looking sloppy; we had a reputation to uphold. Keep in mind the entire time that we were marching, each of us had to be mindful of these elements:

- Keep your shoulders square to the press box.
- No turning your head, and only use your peripheral vision.
- Flute players (that's for me), keep your instrument parallel to the ground. If your shoulders slump, you'll make the band look lazy.
- When marching forward, keep your toes pointed high.
- Roll your feet.
- When marching backward, get up on your tiptoes. If you don't, your feet will stick to the turf; you may fall or cause others to fall.

And those were just the fundamentals! We also had to:

- Memorize sets.
- Remember how many steps were from point A to point B.
- Memorize show music.
- Keep our instruments in tune and if they weren't, we needed to figure that out quickly before stepping on the field.
- Be able to stand at attention.

Standing at attention meant holding our instruments in front of us before we started a show or while we were waiting for instructions from the drum major. I don't think any of us cared for it too much, but it taught us patience and built our endurance. This was especially true when we were standing at the back of a field about to march in the heat and humidity of Texas in the fall. On a typical game day, it could be ninety-five degrees and 100 percent humidity at eight in the evening. Mind you, we were dressed in long black pants, a T-shirt, and a grass green wool coat adorned with gold buttons from 1970-something. In addition to this fashion travesty, we had a black marching helmet with an uncomfortable plastic chin strap. It didn't matter if we had sweat pouring down our faces or a quarter-sized mosquito that just snacked on our pinky finger. We could not move and break "attention."

By the time we reached the state band championship, we could see how much all our hard work had paid off. Standing at attention for twenty-plus minutes felt easy, and we were as polished as any other band competing for the state title. We had "dehydrated" our lazy teen attitudes, our poorly conditioned muscles, and our scattered mindsets. We had our unique patina.

In the summer of 2017, I endured one of the worst pains known to humans—one that takes out athletes and cancels their careers. I blew out my knee with a partially torn MCL, meniscus, and a 100 percent snapped in half ACL. It was a late evening of July fourth weekend. We had gone over to the barn to have my oldest daughter practice riding her new horse. At the time, we knew nothing about picking a horse let alone picking out a horse that was kiddo safe. We bought what we thought was a good one and assumed any little quirk we saw would work itself out. The horse took off with my daughter across the pasture and next thing we hear is, "Mom, mom, mom he won't stop get me off!"

With my momma's heart racing, I ran to the gate to call the horse over to me. Thankfully, her horse Romeo made his way to the gate, and my daughter was still safely in her saddle. She was shaken up but all right. One rule of thumb when owning horses is that when they do something like that, you never want it to be their last ride. You want to correct any behavior mishaps and let that be the way they finish their day.

Not thinking in my fullest capacity, I got on him to work his sporadic attitude out of him until we had a good ride. Mistake number one was not checking the cinch aka the thing that goes around their belly to make sure the saddle is snug against the horse. My second mistake was thinking my adult sized behind was going to fit perfectly fine in my seven-year-old child's saddle. Obviously, I really set myself up for disaster here. We started on our little ride, and everything seemed fine. Then, he wanted to quicken the pace, and from then on, it felt like life was moving in slow motion.

The child size saddle began to glide sideways on his sweaty back and I gave my best effort to readjust it to compensate for the slippage. He had a spurt of energy running through his veins and proceeded to jolt across a small trench. This was all it took. I knew at that point I was going down; I just didn't know in what capacity. After the trench there was a slight turn at the fence where I began to lift out of the saddle and sadly not gracefully. My back hit the fence and my knee rubber-banded from left to right 180 degrees in a matter of a second with a distinctive pop in the joint. It instantly went numb, and I couldn't bare weight on it when I tried to stand. Swelling was immediate in my brand-new cowgirl jeans. Honesty I really wanted to get my jeans off because cowgirl jeans cost about eighty bucks a pop, and I didn't want them cut off at the emergency room.

I put on my friend's shorts, and I was rushed to the nearest ER. After getting the X-rays the doctor determined my leg wasn't broken but given the amount of swelling, he encouraged me to see an orthopedic doctor right away. After my orthopedic appointment and MRI, I was told that my MCL and meniscus were partially torn and that my ACL was completely torn. Surgery was discussed, but I didn't have the emotional or physical support to allow for such an invasive procedure or recovery period. In my thinking, "Mama couldn't be down at all, so she had to keep going forward somehow." I was to go home to rest and recover before any further treatment was permitted. Physical therapy was only going to be allowed after swelling dissipated.

Some weeks later, I no longer had a bubble for my knee and could begin to function normally although I was still unable to bend my leg fully and putting any kind of weight on it was excruciating. At this point I could only bend it to about forty degrees, which is not really anything. I began physical therapy twice a week, but it was painful. This momma had big alligator tears. Surely, I thought, it has to get better than this, right? This place is supposed to make you feel better!

Week after week I went to my therapy sessions with little progress to show for all my hard work. One day, I went in for an appointment exhausted from working all day and hot and miserable. Texas summers are brutal, and our fall season isn't much better. I made my way to the therapy table for my physical therapist to proceed with the electrode treatment. Once she began, out of nowhere I began to cry. It wasn't the cute girl cry either. It was a hot mascara mud streaming down my cheeks kind of cry session. I was so frustrated from hurting physically, mentally, and emotionally that I couldn't hold it in anymore.

Dianne, my physical therapist, didn't even ask what she could do or say anything. She just wrapped her arms around me and gave me the biggest mama bear hug. She sat with me in the ocean of all my hurts. God knew what I needed, and I am so thankful He lined it up in advance for me to be her client. She shared with me she was a believer and would be praying not only for my physical recovery but for my heart too. I have never forgotten that day, and it encourages me when I have hard moments.

There were so many other moments while I was at home doing my exercises when tears spilled over from the pain of working the ligaments and quad muscles. I wanted to quit. A lot. I knew deep down I'd never get better with a thought process like this and besides what kind of example would I be setting for my daughter if I quit? She needed to see that Mama could persevere so that she could have an example of that in her life.

One of the home exercises was especially difficult for me to do. I had to sit on the floor with my legs stretched in front of me and my toes pointed toward the ceiling. Next, I had to take a towel, wrap it around the arch of my foot, and use it to pull my knee slowly toward me to make an angle. Then, as if that wasn't excruciating enough, I had to hold that bent position for at least five seconds and work up to thirty seconds. There were lots of hot tears pouring down my cheeks on a daily basis. It was the most uncomfortable position but also probably the most helpful to regain my muscle strength.

It came to a point in my visits where I needed to begin more resistance training. It's not a bad thing in theory, but in my head my thoughts went something like this, "You have got to be kidding! I can barely walk and now you want me to get on the knee bendy machine thing and try to ride a bicycle?!" My stubborn nature did not want to do it. I even tried to convince my therapist I wasn't ready for the next level of therapy. However, she knew it was necessary since other exercises had become easier for me.

My knee bend had gotten to ninety degrees, but to "pass" physical therapy and to acquire the sign-off from my orthopedic doctor, I needed to be at a 140-degree bend. Each week I increased my capacity with both exercises. I did not see immediate results but gradually over a few months, I was able to hit my goal. My ortho passed me with flying colors and was happy to see I had mostly recovered from my injuries. He ordered a special knee brace to help with stability for certain strenuous activities.

Probably the most important thing I had to learn during this recovery process was the art of giving myself grace. Not one time in my whole thirty-plus years of living had I ever experienced an injury like that one. I also have the propensity to be a lot harder on myself than I need to be. Many times, I wanted to be further along in my physical therapy than I was and when I had setbacks, it frustrated me. It was in those moments of frustration that my character was being refined. Patience and perseverance were building. Little did I know that I would need those skills when I reached the season of going through a divorce and again many times over after that.

God knew the frosted patina I'd have after all the tempered seasons I endured, and He certainly knows what yours will look like too. Paul wrote so beautifully in 2 Corinthians these words of encouragement: *"Therefore we do not lose heart. Though outwardly we are wasting away, yet inwardly we are being renewed day by day"* (2 Corinthians 4:16). You have no idea how close you are to the things you have prayed for. Paul believed to his core that even with all the things we endure, it is still worth it to gain our eternal inheritance.

I am thankful for the times the Lord has used songs and lyrics to speak to my heart, especially when they are biblically based. One in particularly was from Psalm 30:5: *"For his anger lasts only a moment, but his favor lasts a lifetime; weeping may stay for the night, but rejoicing comes in the morning."* I have walked through very difficult seasons when I saw no hope—times when I could not see the possibility of joy arriving. I am so thankful knowing that just because things might not be good, He most definitely isn't done with my situations or yours, not quite yet. God doesn't want us to wallow in our sorrows for too long. He keeps reaching into our souls to encourage us when we want to give up in what we think are hopeless situations.

Keep going, sweet reader, until He's done with it! If things still look bleak, then the rain clouds haven't parted over your waters yet. Your new frosted patina in Christ after your season of tempering is going to be someone else's hope. They need to you to complete your healing just as much as you need it for yourself.

Chapter 10 Journal Prompts

We have done so much work and made progress during our journey together. I am very proud of you for sticking with it and using these prompts to help you to journal. Go back to the list you created in the Chapter 9 prompts and use it below.

1. For this chapter's journal time, take a moment to relish all the victories God has delivered to you. Use this as an opportunity to praise Him for all the work you and God have done together. You worked hard for this. Celebrate!

2. The list you created in Chapter 9 explored ways you felt stronger and healed. From that list, pinpoint the experiences that built those specific aspects that formed the stronger, healed, refined you.

3. Feel free to express your gratitude here for all that God has done. Whether this be with pen and paper, a worship session, art session, or even prayer time. In whatever form or fashion, you would like to express it, take this time to do so.

CHAPTER 11

Counterfeits

To be yourself in a world that is constantly trying to make you something else is the greatest accomplishment.

—Ralph Waldo Emerson

Emerson knew a thing or two when it came to being authentic. He penned letters, essays, and poetry during the Transcendental era of the 1820s and 1830s. He was one of the greatest intellectual minds of his time. In the tradition of our founding fathers, Emerson and others fought against conformity and urged society to be independent to authentically be themselves. One of his most famous essays was titled, *Self-Reliance.* An excerpt from this essay reads as followed:

> Insist on yourself; never imitate. Your own gift you can present every moment with the cumulative force of a whole life's cultivation, but of the adopted talent

of another, you have only an extemporaneous, half possession. That which each can do best, none but his Maker can teach him. No man yet knows what it is, nor can, till that person has exhibited it. Where is the master who could have taught Shakespeare? Where is the master who could have instructed Franklin, or Washington, or Bacon, or Newton? Every great man is a unique.[24]

For every authentic sea glass piece discovered, there is an equal amount that is counterfeit. If rarity is something to be valued, then the enemy will try to distort our worth by any means possible. Since the beginning of mankind, we have had a war waged against our souls to keep us from being successful. At times it almost seems like a divine comedy in which Satan gets pleasure out of watching us falter under the delusion of our sinful natures. If the enemy can get us to undervalue ourselves and misalign our worth against what God's word says about us, then we will destroy ourselves with counterfeit ideals of the truth.

Thus, it is imperative to educate ourselves with God's truth so when the hard times come, which they will, we will be ready to combat the falsehoods. A careful study of the armor of God reveals that the shield is one of our most important defenses. Ephesians 6:16 says, *"In addition to all, taking up the shield of faith with which you will be able to extinguish all the flaming arrows of the evil one."* The shield is the protection needed for us to advance forward. Ancient shields were massive, weighing a hefty twenty-two pounds; soldiers soaked their shields in water so the fiery darts were not able to harm them or their comrades.

The measure of faith you have will be your protective shield against what is waged against you. Please, I beg you, do not give into the lies from the enemy of your soul. Every time the lies start to pour into you, combat them with Scripture.

Lie from the enemy:	What the Lord says:	Scripture to back it up:
I don't need help.	I will tell you the path to take.	Proverbs 3:5–6
This is too much.	If you follow me, I'll help you.	Matthew 11:28–30
No one loves me.	You are loved.	Psalm 86:15
I'm unforgiveable.	You are forgiven.	Colossians 3:13
There is no hope.	There is always hope.	Lamentations 3:20–23
But what if.	I will take care of you.	Philippians 4:19
I feel alone.	I am here for you.	1 Peter 5:7
I can't do this.	You can.	Isaiah 41:10

You should be aware that there are different degrees of healing. There is partial healing, complete healing, and false healing. Partial healing is when you're still working through some things, but you understand that it is a process, which might take months or even years to complete. However, you've recognized the need to heal, and you've committed yourself to do what it takes to achieve your goals. It takes discipline, continued expenditures of resources, and a lot of patience with yourself and the process itself. These resources could be monetary or time.

There are a few things that linger in my journey from the divorce that I am still addressing and moving forward to repair within my heart. I consider this to be my partial healing. Now, I can step back and look over the span of my marriage and own my faults and those of the other party. I have given a tremendous amount of grace and forgiveness to myself and much more to the other party. However, there are deep wounds into which salt has been poured many times—even post-divorce. It is a struggle some days to remember that my worthiness comes only from the Lord, not from what another person says about me. I am still healing from the trauma of someone else's misaligned intimacy desires; I will say that this has been a difficult area for me to find peace in.

I've been working on this with my counselor, and journaling has been most helpful. She told me to pay attention to how my body reacts when I reflect on distressing events. If, for example, a TV program contains certain kinds of scenes, I've had to turn the TV off or walk out of the room. By paying attention to my body, I notice there is an overwhelming tenseness in my muscles and my mind goes back to what happened; I get very quiet, and then I feel like crying for a while afterward.

I am so thankful to be with a wonderfully patient man now—one who values me as a woman and has never put my mind, body, or spirit in a compromised position. He has made sure that I have a safe space within his arms. He sits with me on the couch and lets me cry and talk it out or just be silent. This mirrors the love our God extends to me and everyone as well. He sits with us in our grief, in our healing, in our painful trenches. He doesn't judge us; He doesn't say you should be further down the road in your journey. He also doesn't say, "Let me tell you about your next steps right now." Nope. God sits with us right where we are and lovingly says, "I know. It wasn't fair. Just lean on me in the middle of it. I'll sit with you here as long as you need me to." That's love, sweet reader.

Complete healing is when we have done the hard work within our minds, hearts, and emotions. We have gained a renewed or refreshed sense of peace and understanding. Philippians reminds us of this in 4:7: *"And the peace of God, which surpasses all understanding, will guard your hearts and minds through Christ Jesus."* This often means that our perspective has shifted and that we are able to see the situation or experiences as they are instead of having the emotional distress we did when the experience happened to us.

Typically, complete healing also includes forgiving ourselves and forgiving others. Remember though, forgiveness is for you to reunite your heart to God. There is no need for you to tell someone you've forgiven them. He only instructs us to forgive others as He has forgiven us: *"Be kind and compassionate to one another, forgiving each other, just as in Christ God forgave you"* (Ephesians 4:32). You're releasing the person to the Lord and protector of your heart. Let Him do what He does best, and that's being God. Don't worry either; everything will be balanced in the end, sweet reader, even when it doesn't feel like it will. (I am preaching to myself right here too; trust me!) God has seen the whole situation and struggle from second number one! Apostle Paul says, *"Do not take revenge, my dear friends, but leave room for God's wrath, for it is written: 'It is mine to avenge; I will repay,' says the Lord"* (Romans 12:19).

Forgiveness is not—and I repeat this to you in the boldest way—forgiveness is not to reconcile with someone. Reconciliation is not always possible. That could be due to death, geography, or different life paths and belief systems. Trying to reconcile could mean putting your mental or physical well-being in harm's way if you engaged in a conversation with the offender. Tony Evans says it best in his *Detours* Bible study when he says, "Biblical forgiveness is the decision to no longer credit an offense against an offender with a view of enacting vengeance. It also involves releasing that person from a debt owed as well as the blame that he or she deserves due to an infraction or sin committed against you. Keep in mind, forgiveness is a decision. It is not first and foremost an emotion."[25]

In our mom group, we had a situation in which one of the moms wasn't making very wise life choices. It infuriated me that they would put their child through the things that they did. It also made my mama heart hypersensitive when my child was around them. All sorts of questions and anxious feelings swirled through my mind. At one point there was a falling out with this woman, which eventually led our daughters not being close friends anymore. Things were said about my daughter, my family, and myself; finally, I had had enough of it. This mama bear was poked hard! It took me a long time to forgive the other mom for what she did not only to me but also how she made my daughter feel. In the thick of this season, I felt awful for my daughter losing a close friend. Then the mama guilt came in.

What if I had kept my mouth shut about how I felt about the unsafe situations I was seeing play out? Why did I have to be the voice of reason? Did I do the right thing by putting up some healthy boundaries? What do I do about what felt like retaliation against us for setting boundaries?

And you know what God told me to do after asking these questions? He said to stop worrying about it—that He had it taken care of. Ugh, I cannot tell you how frustrating that answer was; I'm sure you can understand. However, it was indeed the Lord's battle to fight, not mine, and I needed to let it go. About a year later I saw this woman at a school event; she walked around the field and placed her chair right next to mine and said hello. We lightly conversed, and that was it. That was when I realized it was all OK. I saw her as a person God loved and was restoring. She had her life, and I had mine. There was no drama. I felt peaceful and fine; I had complete healing from everything that happened between us.

When I was going through my healing work a few years ago with my counselor, it really surprised me how much unforgiveness I had harbored. There was some with myself, my ex-husband, friends, and even my parents. The years of work I did with my counselor were the most important and valuable work I ever did for myself. Years later, I can see that it was prudent to have done so due to the seasons which followed. That's another story and another book though. I will say there are things I'm still working on. However, as I stated before, some things take a lot of time to heal through.

The fall before I decided to file the petition for divorce, a big disagreement transpired between a good friend and me. When I shared some tough and painful experiences that I had gone through, it was with the mutual understanding that we had each other's back, no matter what. I had a deep level of trust with this friend, and I thought that meant I could be vulnerable with this very sensitive subject. It was something that shook me to my core deeply. I just wanted my few close friends to say in a nutshell, "That is terrible! I hate this happened to you." I wanted them to sit in my trench with me until I felt I could process the situation.

Instead, I was met with a disappointed response, which left me feeling invalidated, and honestly, it felt crippling. I was hurt! How could they tell me to dismiss the situation like that and unfairly judge me by saying that I was being unreasonable with my hurt and sorrow? It felt like I had gotten backhanded with a two-by-four! The hurt remained for several weeks; I felt disconnected from my friend, and it was the first time I had ever felt that with them. I didn't like it. It felt awful. I ended up working through this with my counselor and decided that I needed to put up boundaries around the friendship. What had happened in my marriage was painful. It was hurtful, and if my friend wasn't going to be a safe person for me to talk things through, then a boundary needed to be made. In this instance, I forgave them for how they responded to my hurting heart. We had the hard conversations as old friends often do and worked through the details. At that point, I thought the healing had come and was there to stay like a cozy, warm blanket on a fall day.

However, it wasn't until recently, three years later, that I realized there was still some unforgiveness which was rooted in that season. I discovered that counterfeit healing and forgiveness had taken place. My friend and I had a discussion about current life circumstances and struggles. By the end of our conversation, our emotions were getting the best of the of us, and feelings were getting hurt on both sides. The conversation definitely could have gone better. We had a disagreement about how I handled something, and my friend told me that I was too emotional. That landed me right back how I felt three years ago; I felt like an idiot for letting my guard down and telling this person some of the things I was going through. I had thought I could trust them again with some confidential situations, but with the more recent conversation, I knew I needed to extend grace even though I felt they didn't deserve it.

Looking back at the situation, I felt as though my friend wasn't allowing me to have validated feelings and that I should feel embarrassed to have any emotion about our conversation. I was actually feeling shame. According to Brené Brown, "Shame is the intensely painful feeling or experience of believing that we are flawed and therefore unworthy of love and belonging."[26] Having some years of counseling under my belt, I'm glad I was able to recognize I was triggered by the responses given. It had the same yuck feeling from years prior. I apologized for not handling the conversation well and acknowledged that I should have asked whether it was OK to talk about things I was going through first. There were hurt feelings on both sides. I didn't feel understood, heard, or loved. I think I cried for the rest of the evening and decided that I needed distance and time to work through my unforgiveness.

I needed to realize that my friend was in a different season of life from me altogether; I was divorced, she wasn't. Her kids were young; mine spanned a timeframe of eight years, one of which crossed into teenage years. We had different things on our plates in different capacities. Ultimately, it meant at that time, I needed to give grace even though it was hard. It doesn't mean that how I felt about our conversation was invalid. It did mean that I was healing and could see what needed to happen before it escalated into the end of a long-standing friendship. True forgiveness in my heart was the answer.

In my quest for sea glass, I have learned that the more reliable place to look for genuine pieces is the ocean. That's it. Rarely will you find authentic sea glass in seaside shops. Most of what you find in shops, stores, and even online are fabricated replicas. Genuine pieces are unique in their shape, size, and texture, and their surface can be porous. According to Linda Jereb at By The Sea Jewelry,[27] under a microscope, these tiny porous holes are C-shaped and follow no uniform pattern, making them all unique. Counterfeit sea glass has uniformity in the surface texture, and it is commercially etched with machines.

Faux glass will often have a tumbling residue, and from my experience as a collector, the thickness varies greatly. We have found tiny thin shards as well as pieces that span a couple of inches in width. One thing to keep in mind is that vintage glass tends to be thicker. There's no telling how old some of our pieces are, but oh if they could talk. Linda Jereb offers these tips for confirming the authenticity of sea glass:[28]

- Is it too smooth? Is it too rough?
- Are the geometric shapes all the same?
- Are the rare colors being sold at too low of a price?

A genuine piece of rare red sea glass sold for around $600, and I have other pieces valued at several hundreds of dollars each. In comparison, commercial sea glass sells for a few dollars apiece or on average twenty dollars for a large quantity.

I could easily take a piece of glass and use sandpaper to manufacture my own sea glass. But is that genuine? How long would the faux finish last before it wears off? Only what is authentic and genuine will stand the test and trials of life. The same is true of your healing journey. Don't allow a counterfeit spirit to overtake your heart. You deserve a genuine healing no matter how much time the voyage takes.

Chapter 11 Journal Prompts

Sometimes, our healing can feel complete when it really isn't. This could be a product of false teachings put there by others or ourselves.

1. Are there any counterfeits in your life? This could be in the form of false teachings, misbelief, or toxic things we have put in our hearts or that others have.

2. How can you combat these things? (If it is a spiritual battle versus an internal battle, take the time here to call out the enemy's game plan, which is to have you live in an unworthy state of mind. In Romans 8:37, God called you to be a conqueror. Praise wins the battle; remember that. Your Jericho will fall with praise during the battle.)

CHAPTER 12

Found from Reflection

For whatever we lose (like a you or a me), it's always our self we find in the sea.

— E. E. Cummings

Sea glass can be found but only if one knows where to look. After the very first time my oldest daughter and I found a piece of sea glass, I knew from that day forward I wanted to make it our thing. It was like our own little treasure hunt. We had gone out that morning for a fishing trip; however, the attention span of a six-year-old will only stretch so far. I had no intention of finding anything. To be frank, I had no idea that sea glass was something we could find in our area. At best, the treasures we had found up to that point were seashells, hermit crabs, and red seaweed.

I packed our fishing gear into my vehicle, and we went on a scavenger hunt adventure for seashells. The area where we were had a decent shoreline, but what we were finding was less than ideal for my little "Shells." I should explain that my daughter's name is Shelby, but we coined the nickname for her around the time she picked up her first shell.

Earlier that morning, we had passed a rocky area near the shoreline. I thought surely there should be something she's looking for over there. I parked and much to our delight there were hundreds of seashells. There were white ones, colored ones, and ones with swirled curlicues draped across the sea enamel. There were even several with a beautiful iridescent purple lining painted against a smooth shell surface. About half of my daughter's collection cup was filled with purple ones. As we continued to shell hunt, a faint reflection caught my eye. Much to my surprise, it was a beautiful, perfectly frosted piece of sea glass. From that day forward, every time we go to that spot we always stop to see if there are any pieces waiting for us to take home.

Sea glass is easier to find when it's sunny because the light is reflected off the pieces.[29] It is much harder to find with the shadows of a dimmed sunset and encroaching evening sky—but not impossible. It's just a little more difficult to find. The sea glass becomes hidden by the shadows cast by a mid-summer sunset or darkened just enough to blend into the rocks around it. I would like to interject one sliver of hope right here: God is never late. Your hope will be found at the exact moment you need it. Ecclesiastes reminds us of this in 3:11: *"Yet God has made everything beautiful for its own time. He has planted eternity in the human heart, but even so, people cannot see the whole scope of God's work from beginning to end"* (NLT).

I have found that seasons after major life changes or events are either joyful or the most difficult. After my fourth miscarriage, I thought for sure we would never have more children. I had several blood tests run over the course of a few years and learned that I had PCOS (polycystic ovarian syndrome), which made it extremely difficult for me to conceive. My doctors also told me that even if I had a cycle, it didn't mean that I was ovulating. That is, just because my body was menstruating, there might not be an egg available for fertilization. My body was basically in a misfire mode. In addition, once my body became pregnant, I had another condition that stacked all odds against our little baby's survival. I also had a protein-c deficiency, which caused my body to clot heavily only during pregnancy causing micro clots to enter the blood supply to the baby. This would eventually cut off the blood supply to our baby causing me to miscarry. I was absolutely devastated when I got the answers to all of my whys, but it did offer some clarification.

The first loss was in the spring of 2014. About a month after the pregnancy test confirmation in the doctor's office, red spots began to show up. I immediately called my doctor and was told to come in for an examination. My heart was racing, and my vision was blurred from anxiousness. In that moment she confirmed my body was going to miscarry. Not only this, even though my body was twelve weeks pregnant, the egg was empty. I asked, "Are you absolutely sure?" She said yes, the blood test and ultrasound confirmed the same results. There was a genetic complication that caused the incomplete formation. She told me if I didn't start to miscarry naturally then I needed to come back for a procedure called a D&C. What was even worse, the following weekend was my sister-in-law's baby shower. I felt obligated to attend, but I needed to leave soon after my arrival.

I didn't want to rain on her happy celebration, nor could I physically continue. I left the shower weeping as my body had started to heavily miscarry. The physical pain was enough to take my breath away as I began my thirty-minute drive home. I didn't want to talk to anyone. I just wanted to sit in my dark bedroom and weep my heavy tears. Three more miscarriages would follow with more testing in October 2015, June 2016, and December 2016. My faith was shaken, and I was equally done with saying to everyone, "I'll be fine." I wanted to be more than "just fine." I wanted to feel hopeful, peaceful, and joyful again.

It took a very long time to heal my heart from the heavy grief of losing my babies, and the heaviest burden of all was feeling like it was my fault. The more I talked about it, the more I sought after healing. The more I sought healing, that's when the blessings came. The blessing of peace, the blessing of comfort knowing I wasn't alone in my grief or suffering. I had begun to hear stories from other women in and out of my circle about their experiences with recurring losses. These women were my people. God was giving me a community of people to share my sorrow with. Scripture was coming to life for me and the lie of, "No one understands what I'm going through," was being shattered!

It was a counterfeit to what Scripture says to be true. I felt isolated in my brokenness, and I believed I was alone in my grief. I'd say for about five years, I felt this way. Little did I know that having a miscarriage was more prevalent than I thought. The common thread from all the women I spoke with was that they all felt alone. They all believed the lie just like I did. Right then and there, our belief in it was exposed when we called it out. God was with us in our sorrows, and we gained strength from each other. Two Scriptures that comforted me during these tough times were out of Psalms and Romans. They were the warm spiced tea I needed during my bitter cold mourning:

- *"The LORD is close to the brokenhearted and saves those who are crushed in spirit"* (Psalm 34:18).
- *"Rejoice with those who rejoice; mourn with those who mourn"* (Romans 12:15).

Now trust me, I was angry for a long time in addition to my sorrow. I questioned God relentlessly it seemed. I asked things like, why did you take them away? Why did you allow such a cruel joke to be played with my heart? Why four times? Why not just leave it at one? I felt even more angry because I did not feel like God was listening or caring about my mama heart at all. I felt distant from Him and felt bitterness begin to poison my hope like sticky tar. I may not ever fully comprehend God's reasoning for allowing my losses, but I do know He has a purpose for it all. I have been able to use my hurt to encourage others when they have faced secondary infertility or miscarriages. I found my healing from within the reflection of my pain, which revealed hope to not only other women but also to myself.

There is one other time when I have found it is easier to find our little treasures of the sea. It comes right after a rainstorm. The dusty sand is swept away or dampened. Rocks become saturated and darkened with raindrops falling from a heavy sky. Even though the sunlight radiates through the storm clouds at an eclipsed rate, there is usually enough for one's eyes to adjust for sea glass hunting.

I scan the ground, and the dampness provides the perfect contrast for colors to pop amongst the rocks and sand. In art, contrast is important because it allows the eye to be guided to a focal point with ease. It also highlights the important things the artist is trying to convey to the viewer. The differences between light and dark become quite clear in this manner, and the dampness offers a reflective surface for the sun rays to bounce off. Usually, I can find things at an accelerated rate this way. Just last night I went to the shoreline after a rain shower and found seven pieces within ten minutes. The opaque pieces were no longer halfway hidden and were there for all the world to find.

Sometimes, the beautiful things of our healing are found during the sunny times in our lives. Everything is going good in our work and personal lives, and it propels or motivates us to keep on going. Other times, those beautiful things are found after the storms—storms of disobedient children, health diagnosis, hurt from a friend, inner struggles, and the list can go on from here. Though the elements surrounding the moments of discovery may be vastly different, one thing remains the same. Every time I found pieces of sea glass, it was because light was present. This same ideal applies for us. Light must be present for things to be refracted back for our discovery.

Ephesians 5:13 says, *"But everything exposed by the light becomes visible—and everything that is illuminated becomes a light."* I want you to know not one part of your life has been for nothing. Not one heartache, one tear, one experience, or one minute of discouragement. Though moments in your life may have been difficult or hurtful, remember He isn't going to waste your pain.

Every raindrop that falls from the laden sky exposes more rock and more refracted light up to my eye to catch the glimmer of sea treasures beneath my feet. It's the same with your tears, love. Every tear exposes the things God wants to refract back to you—things that have been beneath your feet the whole time. Our tears end up being the irrigation system to our greatest blessings. It's hard to even begin to believe this when you're in the thick of it, trust me. To have a fruitful garden, water is the key element for growth.

What areas of your life need reflection into your heart to find your hope? Your peace? Your healing? Your stolen years that people, the enemy, or even you took from yourself? It is all there I promise you. Digging through the rocks of our hearts allows healing to wash ashore. Even if your eyes are closed when the water comes to wash things against you, it's OK. You're still present. That's all that matters.

Sweet reader, that is the only way that healing comes. Warmth begins to thaw our wounds when the light of Jesus shines onto our hidden broken pieces. We only delay our healing when we keep it all covered up or when we decline to step into the water to be present with what is washing away and washing ashore.

I love the story of when Jesus calls Peter to him whilst at sea. To set the scene a little bit here, right before these men were in a boat on a lake-like sea, they had just witnessed a full-blown miracle. Jesus took five loaves of bread and two fish and multiplied them to feed five thousand men plus all their wives and children. I'll let you do the math here, but that's more than five thousand mouths to feed:

> *When Jesus heard what had happened, he withdrew by boat privately to a solitary place. Hearing of this, the crowds followed him on foot from the towns. When Jesus landed and saw a large crowd, he had compassion on them and healed their sick. As evening approached, the disciples came to him and said, "This is a remote place, and it's already getting late. Send the crowds away, so they can go to the villages and buy themselves some food."*
>
> *Jesus replied, "They do not need to go away. You give them something to eat."*
>
> *"We have here only five loaves of bread and two fish," they answered.*
>
> *"Bring them here to me," he said. And he directed the people to sit down on the grass. Taking the five loaves and the two fish and looking up to heaven, he gave thanks and broke the loaves. Then he gave them to the disciples, and the disciples gave them to the people. They all ate and were satisfied, and the disciples picked up twelve basketfuls of broken pieces that were left over. The number of those who ate was about five thousand men, besides women and children.*
>
> —Matthew 14:13–21

In addition, the blessing of multiplied food was so great there were leftovers! It is not clear as to what happened to the extra food specifically, other than the disciples taking it. However, the biggest thing I see after reading these Scriptures is that the disciples had physical, tangible evidence to reinforce the miracle that had just taken place. I believe it was a tool Jesus used to increase their faith because He already knew what was coming in the hours that would follow. They needed that padding of faith so when the test that could possibly shake their world unfolded, it wouldn't.

The story as Jesus instructed the disciples to travel across the Sea of Galilee in a wooden fishing boat. Meanwhile, Jesus stayed behind to send the gathering of people home. By our understanding of the difference between a sea and a lake, we would say that this body of water was more of a lake spanning thirteen miles long and seven miles wide. However, it was subject to sudden squalls during certain times of the year. After Jesus sent everyone away, He went up to the mountain to pray. I cannot help but picture Jesus having his quiet time with the Father, only to look down at the sea and shaking his head with frustration at the disciples' lack of faith. Scripture says that a storm came upon them. Matthew 14:24 says, *"But the ship was now in the midst of the sea, tossed with waves: for the wind was contrary."*

The Bible tells us Jesus went down to the sea and walked on it. The disciples are anxious, scared, and trembling with fear because they had no idea what or who was out on the water. Jesus recognized their fear:

> *And in the fourth watch of the night Jesus went unto them, walking on the sea. And when the disciples saw*

> *him walking on the sea, they were troubled, saying, It is a spirit; and they cried out for fear. But straightway Jesus spake unto them, saying, Be of good cheer; it is I; be not afraid.*
>
> —Matthew 14:25–27 KJV

I would most definitely be questioning my sanity at this point, and my heart would have been beating nearly out of my chest. I cannot say my reaction would have been any different from that of the disciples.

This next part of this story is what is so awesome to me. Peter was the only one who spoke up saying, "Lord, if it's you," Peter replied, "tell me to come to you on the water" (Matthew 14:28). There was something inside Peter that had grown exponentially from the things he just witnessed hours prior. It made his soul know that the guy in front of him was his Lord, his future Savior and was reflecting back the same Spirit He had. This was Jesus! Before Peter knows it, his feet were over the side of the boat walking toward Jesus. However, in a moment of human rationality, he began to allow fear to overtake him once the wind picked up. His natural senses were telling him, "You're going to drown; you're so many feet above solid ground with water dangerously about to engulf your body."

We find in Matthew 14:28–33 that walking on water wasn't rational for Peter's mind to comprehend, so he began to sink:

> *And he [Jesus] said, Come. And when Peter was come down out of the ship, he walked on the water, to go to Jesus. But when he saw the wind boisterous, he was*

> *afraid; and beginning to sink, he cried, saying, Lord, save me. And immediately Jesus stretched forth his hand, and caught him, and said unto him, O thou of little faith, wherefore didst thou doubt? And when they were come into the ship, the wind ceased. Then they that were in the ship came and worshipped him, saying, Of a truth thou art the Son of God.*
>
> —Matthew 14:29–33 KJV

Jesus recognized that His disciples still needed to increase their faith. I believe it was from what He was seeing reflected out of their actions during the storm. Perhaps this is why once they reach shore and meet another multitude of people, Jesus again feeds thousands of people. He wanted to prove to them again that He really was who He said He was. This part of the story can be found in Chapter 15 of Matthew:

> *Jesus left there and went along the Sea of Galilee. Then he went up on a mountainside and sat down. Great crowds came to him, bringing the lame, the blind, the crippled, the mute and many others, and laid them at his feet; and he healed them. The people were amazed when they saw the mute speaking, the crippled made well, the lame walking and the blind seeing. And they praised the God of Israel.*
>
> *Jesus called his disciples to him and said, "I have compassion for these people; they have already been with me three days and have nothing to eat. I do not want to send them away hungry, or they may collapse on*

> *the way." His disciples answered, "Where could we get enough bread in this remote place to feed such a crowd?"*
>
> *"How many loaves do you have?" Jesus asked. "Seven," they replied, "and a few small fish." He told the crowd to sit down on the ground. Then he took the seven loaves and the fish, and when he had given thanks, he broke them and gave them to the disciples, and they in turn to the people. They all ate and were satisfied. Afterward the disciples picked up seven basketfuls of broken pieces that were left over. The number of those who ate was four thousand men, besides women and children. After Jesus had sent the crowd away, he got into the boat and went to the vicinity of Magadan.*
>
> —Matthew 15:29–39

We see here again that Jesus presents them with yet another opportunity to increase their faith. He was still patient with them. Not one time did he tell them, "Really guys?! Are you so ignorant that you can't see it's all going to work out in the end?!" It doesn't matter how many times we have to sail across stormy seas or walk around a mountain. Jesus meets us where we are. He comes to us just like He did with the disciples on the water.

The book of Luke shares the story of Zechariah and Elizabeth who would become the parents of John the Baptist. The blessing of a child seemed like a far-off dream, which would never come to fruition. She was in her eighties by the time she delivered the baby the Lord had promised. His word did not return void! And hear this, sweet reader, it cannot! The Lord is not a liar and per his word in Isaiah, the Lord always keeps his promises! *"So is my word that goes out from my mouth: It will not return to me empty, but will accomplish what I desire and achieve the purpose for which I sent it"* (Isaiah 55:11).

The reflection Elizabeth had in her life from the Lord, mirrored into her son John. With such a high calling on John's life to pave the way for Jesus, the Lord knew this was the family that John needed to be born into. Her pregnancy was a miracle because she had been barren for a long time. If God can fulfill such a promise to her, then he can certainly deliver yours to you despite what is impossibly stacked against you. Take heart in this Scripture, *"Blessed is she who has believed that the lord would fulfill his promises to her"* (Luke 1:45)!

If the waves of the sea or the wind from God's divine hands would not have moved the sediment, we would have never seen the beautiful sea glass just under the surface. The sunlight hit the pieces at the proper angle at the right time. Your beautiful things, such as healing, release, and peace are much closer than you think. When the time is right, I truly believe God will allow your beautifully aligned pieces to be recognizable to your spirit with that lovingly subtle nudge that He gives us. They are right under the surface waiting to be found from your healed reflection.

Chapter 12 Journal Prompts

As I shared in this chapter, it is easier to find sea glass when it is sunny than when the light is dim. God shines the light in places so things can be revealed to us in His timing.

1. What have you discovered by reflecting on the journey you've taken?

2. Where do you feel like you are in your refinement?

3. Do some places still need more time to be tossed back for more "ocean time"?

The Sea Glass Soul

CHAPTER 13

Intrinsic Value

Your life has intrinsic value, not simply because of who you are as an individual, but because of who He is as your God.
—Hannah Anderson

Intrinsic value is a measure of what an asset is worth. The value is calculated by finding the difference between the current price and the value of the strike price. The strike price is the amount at which something can be sold and is otherwise known as the "actual price." The formula for calculating intrinsic value looks like this: $IV = |S-K|$ where IV represents intrinsic value, S equals strike price, and K represents the current value.[30]

In the investment world, knowing this information can help investors understand the value of an asset before purchasing it. Investors want to know if something is overvalued or undervalued with regard to comparable assets.

We can put ourselves into this formula quite easily. First off, this is something I believe we do subconsciously all the time. We compare our current state, situations, and selves against what we think our value is. Sometimes, the difference between the two values is balanced, but I have found that sometimes it is not. How often have you compared yourself against what you thought your value or worth should be? Did you come up short? Did you find balance or equal amounts? Or did you have a surplus of confidence in your value? The result of this equation varies and is incredibly unpredictable.

Other times, we may find ourselves calculating the difference between our current value and the world's current value of us. Most of the time, with this application of the formula, we will feel a deficit. I will never forget one time in middle school when I started to use this formula myself. Middle school is an excruciatingly difficult and awkward stage of life. There are so many fast-paced changes, self-discoveries, and students who are not very kind at that age. As stated previously, middle school was a difficult season for my family. My mother was very ill, and we weren't sure how long she was going to make it. My father worked two jobs, and I was stuck in the trenches of being a girl with grown-up responsibilities. Some of those responsibilities were put on my shoulders because there were no other options. Between my brother and me, I was older. By default, I was handed various chores and caretaking responsibilities.

There were many other things I had put on myself. For instance, I frequently told myself that I had to be a "good" person all the time, and that I had to be on time and always have a plan and think ahead for every detail or scenario. This was my control-coping mechanism because internally, I felt out of control. It felt like I was drowning in a vacant pool with no spectators to see me plummeting to the bottom. Looking back, I barely even saw myself. I didn't understand the value of rest or that I was worthy enough to have healthy boundaries for myself. I didn't know I had a choice. If I could go back, I would tell myself that it is OK to not carry adult responsibilities all the time. Back then, I felt that I had to constantly press forward no matter what. Perseverance isn't a bad quality, but it's not a sustainable lifestyle. Now that I'm an adult, rest has become a very precious necessity and sacred commodity.

During my years of puberty, my hormones were not very kind to me. I had a terrible bout of cystic acne breakouts. All my life, I heard old wives' tales about it, such as, you're eating too much chocolate, you're not eating enough greens, or you must have too much sugar in your diet. My dermatologist tried many different medications, but it got to the point that an experimental drug regiment was the only thing left to try. It was so powerful that my parents would have had to sign a waiver for me to even be on it. The possible side effects were organ damage and infertility. After a long discussion with my parents, we decided the severe health risks were not worth trying the medication. I pushed forward to try to see myself as a beautiful person even if others didn't think I was on the outside. I struggled with insecure feelings about my skin and never thought I was good enough to fit into what I thought was a "normal" teenager body. In high school, I didn't even go to my project graduation or our class trip because I didn't think anyone would notice or care. Internally, I wanted to be seen and connect with my peers, but I believed the lie that I wasn't worthy enough for community.

Turning the dial back to middle school, I remember all the crushes I had—the ones that make your heart flutter when you see that super cute guy from the baseball team. I never felt I would have a chance with him since he was in the popular crowd. So, I convinced myself to be OK with that. What crushed me though wasn't the difference in our social circle; it was what I accidentally overheard. As I headed out the band hall door after school, I saw the cute guy I had a crush on talking to his friend. Too frightened to walk out the door for fear I would be seen, I decided to stay by the door for a few minutes. What I heard next stuck with me for a long time until I learned for myself truly what a beautiful person I was inside and out. The guy's friend said, "That Jamie girl likes you, but she's so ugly with her pizza face there's no way you'd want to be seen with someone like that." The guy looked mortified with the information, and they walked away continuing to talk.

I wanted to run to the back of the band hall and hide for the rest of my life. I never wanted to come out of the dark cold room until either I had no acne or death was upon me to help me escape the embarrassment of being a teen in puberty. The band hall had a vending machine, and I used my leftover lunch money to find temporary comfort in a tasty bit of chocolate, which is my comfort food of choice, up there with my favorite pizza place in my hometown. I thought I was only kidding myself for believing I could have a normal secure life; back then, I never saw myself having what I have now in my late thirties. Eventually, I'd had to seep back into the world from the band hall instrument room and face the facts. The world didn't see my value, and I was losing the little bit I thought I had.

INTRINSIC VALUE

I believed the words spoken that day; then all the doubt flooded in—one lie from the enemy at a time. Questions in my mind populated faster than ants being struck by water. How could I ever be worthy of being called beautiful? How could I ever be seen as desirable to someone? Did the friends I have really like me, or were they just pretending because they felt sorry for the life circumstances I was in and my dotted skin? If God loves me so much, then why on earth did He curse me with such appalling skin? Did God love me at all, or was I ugly to him too?

I was in a heart deficit, and my value had shifted into negative numbers. During high school, I dated a guy who was really the bottom of the barrel. He told me wonderful things, but his heart wasn't in line with the Lord. I thought this must be all that I can get being a little ugly duckling. Let's just say I saw the light eventually of his true character, and I thank God every day for keeping me safe. I'm also thankful to Him for getting me out of situations before I was stuck. The Lord most definitely provided a way out! I am also very thankful for the prayers my parents, youth pastor, and good people who prayed over me while I was in a relationship with this young guy. I know now what they saw and can see how much their prayers made a difference.

God has shown me that my value comes from Him alone. I am worthy of good things because He says so. I have high value because His word declares it over my life and my home. Proverbs 3:15 says, *"She is more precious than rubies; nothing you desire can compare to her."* As much as God knows this, so does our enemy. God knew my calling was writing and that one of my spiritual gifts is encouragement. I have received such clarity given all the things I have lived through, about how much the enemy did and does not want my purpose to come to fruition. This is why I've struggled with discouragement, crippling insecurity, fear, anxiety, and low self-worth and value. The enemy doesn't want me to be successful. He doesn't want me to believe I'm valuable and courageous, and he does not want me to understand that I e am worthy of blessings.

Show yourself where you're being attacked continually, and it will show you where your God-given destiny is. I now understand why I had relationships of poor quality—why I let people walk all over me because I was scared to stand up for myself. Because of the enemy's lies, I had poor boundaries for people. Instead of setting healthy boundaries, I tried to please people or serve them as my way of getting them to love me. After many hurts, I was also anxious about getting too close to people. I was tired of being let down, disappointed, and left. This mentality eventually led me to believe it was easier to do everything myself instead of relying on someone else, even God.

Fear also kept me from pursuing my dream and calling of writing even though I knew from a very young age that I was meant to be a writer. I also knew, this meant I'd be stepping out of my comfort zone and eventually getting in front of people to discuss my writings, speak at events, or hold workshops. My fear of speeches and presentations was debilitating; I would almost black out when I got in front of people. It made so nervous that I put my dreams in a little box, wound it tightly with twine, and said God you've got the wrong girl. Even now, I've found myself thinking at times He could have picked someone better, more qualified, or more experienced.

INTRINSIC VALUE

The commonly threaded themes in my life have been fear, anxiety and discouragement. I am the one who delayed my destiny but let me tell you this woman is on fire for it now! Even though I took the longer routes, otherwise known as my detours, God is still using it all for His purposes. I did a Bible study recently about Joseph and so enjoyed the series about his journey. What I got from it was this: If God can take all the different detours Joseph had in his life and still get him to where he needed to be, then he certainly can do the same thing for me and you.

Joseph was the youngest of his eleven jealous brothers. He hadn't done anything wrong except become their father's favorite child. When he was seventeen, his brothers were so filled with envy that they were determined to kill him. They decided it would be too cruel to kill him, and instead, they tossed him into a pit to perish at nature's hand. However, Midianite merchants traveling close by discovered Joseph, and his brothers sold him into slavery for a mere twenty pieces of silver. In modern times this would be equivalent to about two hundred dollars. During his time in his owner's home, he was falsely accused of a crime and thrown into prison. God allowed him to gain favor in the prison with the very man who threw him in there. While he was in prison, Joseph was put in charge of the all the prisoners! As two of the prisoners were set free, Joseph asked them not to forget about him as he hoped they would put in a good word and help him gain his release. The Lord gifted him with being able to interpret dreams and eventually this set him up to be in high honorable places. Pharaoh got word of this gifting and had Joseph brought to him from prison. Pharaoh had some very off-putting dreams and was confused by what they meant. Not only did Joseph interpret these dreams, but Genesis 41 says Pharaoh put Joseph in charge of all the land.

There wasn't a background check or any second guesses. He barely knew Joseph, but he trusted him with his whole kingdom. When the famines came upon the land, Joseph was the one in charge of rationing out food to the people.

Little did his brothers know, when it was their turn next in the food line that they'd see their brother in this high position. Joseph, the one they had sold into slavery years prior was now delivering their life-giving blessing. Joseph was faithful during all his trials, his valley moments; even at Joseph's very worst, God still saw his value. He knew way before Joseph did what the end goal was. It was to put him in places that he could not have envisioned when he was thrown into that pit to perish.

God didn't give me the idea for this book during a fresh fall morning when I was sitting on my back porch with coffee in hand. There wasn't a joyful sunrise painting of the horizon to enlighten my soul with the words, "Write this book, my beloved Jamie." Oh no. He woke me up in the middle of the night when my heart was broken, and I was in the middle of an inner struggle to file the petition for divorce. I woke up around two or three in the morning with a still, small whisper saying, get up to worship. I wrestled with Him a bit before I stumbled down the hallway half asleep to the living room. I turned on the television and flipped to the YouTube app to find some worship music. I didn't want to disturb the rest of my household, so I turned it down low. As I began to worship, big alligator tears burned my cheeks as they slid down to the rug. I sat like this for nearly an hour. I turned off the music and sat in the quiet of just me and God in the middle of my living room floor. The word *write* was given to me.

I wasn't sure where this was going at that point, so I grabbed a nearby journal and a pen from my desk. I sat back down on the floor and again the word *write* was given to me. I'm like write what, Lord?! Do you want me to write, "I'm crying" on the paper? After sitting a little while longer and repenting for getting a little frustrated, I felt his warm peace knowing that God understood where I was. Then everything started to flow easily. The words for this book title came to me, then the subtitle, then all the chapters and what they'd be about. I looked at the words I had written, and it was if God had taken my hand and had penned the words on my parchment.

To set the scene for you, I had been in counseling for myself and my marriage for nearly two years. The biggest thing I had gained was discovering my worth and understanding my value. I felt empowered, free, and courageous, and I could feel the change within me continually developing. God didn't deliver the message to write when things were good; He delivered it to me when I was in my valley—when the trenches of my warfare were thick as thieves with strongholds and old mindsets breaking off me. He met me in my despair and simply asked me to worship and be obedient. That's when He delivered the map for the next part of my journey. Just like Joseph, all the detours in my life started to make sense.

I understand why I had to be pressed from all sides. Diamonds are only made when immense pressure is present. I was going to be set apart in my job and later be put in positions that required perseverance. I understand why I needed to learn what my value and worth were. This was gained knowledge I would have to pass onto my daughters as this world grows dimmer and darker with its faults, which it will deploy into their futures. Finally, I was needed to be healed so that new things could grow, and love could flourish in my heart once more. Weeds have to be pulled out, so the beautiful things can grow. They also have to be pulled, so the world can also see what did grow.

In the fall of 2023, my twenty-year high school reunion came and went. It was really quite a reflective time. We've lost some good people; I've traveled the world, had two beautiful girls, and gained an encyclopedia of eclectic knowledge. Even with all the things I've endured, I wouldn't have changed a thing. I didn't stay for the entire reunion as I had to pick up my daughters, but several of my friends did. My best friend called to tell me about a comment someone had made about me. My first instinct was to shrivel with anxiety as I used to do when I'd hear something like this. Who in the whole class could have noticed me back then and now at our reunion? Curiosity bested me, and I was intrigued. I put my thoughts at bay and listened.

The comments said were, "Wow, Jamie has really blossomed. She is a beautiful person inside and out. You can see how radiant her skin is, and how she's come into her own self and what joy she has now." This came from a woman I didn't think even noticed the pimple-faced little Jamie back in the day. Regardless of whether my skin cleared or not, I was glad to hear that the work He has done in me was showing outwardly. My dearest sweet best friend replied, "You don't know the hell she has been through or all her struggles. But yes, she sure is doing great now."

INTRINSIC VALUE

The only equation that matters is the one with God in it. He sees our current state and takes everything about us into account—our personality, our experiences, our circumstances, our value we put on ourselves . . . all of it. The biggest difference with the intrinsic value equation is when we put in God's strike value; remember this is the actual value of an asset; the intrinsic value is never ever in a shortage.[31] He strikes out our current value so that the only value left is His, the intrinsic value. Nothing else matters. This equation is never in a deficit, it never changes, and it is never unpredictable.

Every lie about ourselves is torn down. Every criticism is depleted, and everything is set right and balanced. Isaiah 43:4 says, *"Since you are precious and honored in my sight and because I love you, I will give people in exchange for you, nations in exchange for your life."* He loves you so much that He'd give nations for you. You have this much immeasurable worth.

The jar of sea glass my girls and I have collected over the years has grown from a handful of pieces to a whole dairy mason jar full. In fact, when my boss went on vacation to Geneva, she picked up some sea glass pieces for me; I put those pieces in their own little jar. I'm so thankful for all our little treasures from the ocean. Every piece is unique in shape, size, patina, and clarity, and they each have their own travel story. I wish I could have the opportunity to interview each little one about their travels. Where did they come from? A shipwreck from centuries ago? Or perhaps even long-lost message bottles? Trash turned into treasure even? Better yet, maybe they were encapsulated by a hurricane and tossed into the sea. Whatever their story is, if the pieces could talk, I surely would listen.

The Sea Glass Soul

A wonderful woman by the name of April Knecht[32] frequents her nearby beaches to find little treasures. She's been a collector far longer than my daughters and I have been, but our love for sea glass is mutual. She has created wonderful references that one can evaluate their collections by their rarity and colors. April has most definitely done her due diligence here. If you'd like to see the colors broken down, please feel free to visit her webpage at www.realseaglass.com. Perhaps you can check your mason jars to see what kind of sea glass you have sitting on your shelf. Rarity ranges from ultra rare to very limited. The wonder of colors entrances my mind as to what the sea can produce from shattered pieces of previous vessels. The jars on my shelves range from teals, royal blues, aquas, ambers, and even more hues than the heart could imagine. Sea glass can also be graded according to the authentic quality of the piece. Most collectors will have an assortment ranging from perfect to good.

No matter what the rarity, grade, or current price of our collection is, the pieces will always be priceless to me. I was the finder, the investor, the capitalist if you will. I traded my time for memories in finding them. So, the intrinsic value will always be treasured. I'd like to think when I'm gone from this earth, my daughters will continue this tradition with their families one day.

There is an authentic uniqueness with sea glass, which runs parallel to our lives. We develop coarse edges that force us to cut through the waves of life one storm at a time. In hindsight, we've slashed recklessly into others or ourselves. It can feel at times that we are lost amongst our oceans of hurt or experiences. As time moves forward, we are nestled among rocky pebbles and may find it difficult to be dislodged. Eventually, God uncovers us from the shoreline of pain, and we are found from reflection by Him. The difference is He doesn't collect us to be put on display inside mason jars on top of a bathroom armoire. Instead, He holds us. He says, "Look at my beautiful and courageous child. You've made it into my palms of peace. Let me hold you. Let me warm your cold patina surfaces. Let me replace the misbeliefs you've thought about yourself with divine worthiness. I'll hold you and show you the world from my perspective while being nestled safely within the comfort of my loving arms."

Sweet reader, I don't know your ocean story, but God does. It is painted with beautiful colors you haven't even seen yet. Perhaps it's colored with sapphire blues, soft purples, or ribbons of wispy pinks. Or maybe it's illuminated with shades of navy, rich apricot oranges, or vibrant lemonlike yellows. Either way, you are just as unique and timeless as the sunsets in the sky. We each have a story to tell just as these little sea glass treasures do. You're going to overcome the waves send to drown you. You're going to rise up from the water refreshed with strength so powerful that it will be a testimony for someone else's hurricane. While you may not know all the answers to your whys until the other side of Heaven, it is my deepest prayer that you will find peace that passes understanding all throughout your sea glass soul.

Chapter 13 Journal Prompts

You've made it to the end! I'm so joyful about your willingness to stay consistent throughout the journey of refinement. Some places may still take a little more time. Please don't feel bad about this whatsoever. We are all works in progress that are ever-changing, growing, and maturing.

Use this last chapter's prompts to be joyful, celebrate, and encourage yourself to be the best version of yourself. God values you because you are made in His image. I pray and hope you never ever forget that. You are authentically unique.

1. How has your viewpoint changed in comparison to the beginning of our journey together?

Intrinsic Value

2. Do you see the same value that your creator did when He made you?

3. If you had to describe your unique value, what would you say about yourself? (Don't be bashful about talking about yourself here. I personally have a hard time doing so, but as long as it's not in a prideful manner, feel free to express all you'd like to here.)

I have one last thing for you—a commission, if you will. You have traveled with me through these chapters faithfully. You have done the work to become the best version of yourself that you can be. I have one final question for you . . .

4. How can you help others refine their hearts and uncover their value from their broken pieces and shorelines of pain?

References

1. Robin Bertram, *No Regrets: How Loving Deeply and Living Passionately Can Impact Your Legacy Forever* (Charisma House, 2017).
2. Hobart M. King, "Color in Glass," Geology, accessed June 10, 2021, https://geology.com/articles/color-in-glass.shtml.
3. Tim De Jong, Personal Interview. Wimberly Glass Works, June 18, 2023.
4. Brené Brown, *The Gifts of Imperfection* (Hazelden Publishing, 2020), ebook, page 35.
5. Frank Billingsley, "1000 Year Floods? Let's Get Real," Click to Houston, last updated August 26, 2022, 9:46 am., https://www.click2houston.com/weather/2022/08/26/1000-year-floods-lets-get-real/.
6. "Hurricane Harvey's Devastation," California Flood Protection Board, accessed December 28, 2023, https://cvfpb.ca.gov/news/hurricane-harveys-devastation-like-katrinas-again-focuses-attention-on-californias-flood-history-and-need-for-better-preparation-and-protection/ /.

7. Greg Salguerio, "How Much Sodium a Day Do You Need?" Lifespan, July 1, 2020, https://www.lifespan.org/lifespan-living/how-much-sodium-day-do-you- need#:~:text=The%20Institute%20of%20Medicine%20(IOM,mg%20of%20sodium%20per%20day.

8. Monique Warren, "Why Horses Need Salt & Why Salt Blocks Are Not Enough," TheHayPillow.com, August 10, 2020, https://www.thehaypillow.com/blogs/news/why-horses-need-salt-why-salt-blocks-are-not-the-answer.

9. Adrienne Santos-Longhurst, "Can Washing Your Face with Salt Water Really Give You Beach-Fresh Skin?" Heathline, March 15, 2022, https://www.healthline.com/health/washing-face-with-salt-water#takeaway.

10. NOAA, Why Is the Ocean Salty? Ocean Service NOAA, accessed November 11, 2023, https://oceanservice.noaa.gov/facts/whysalty.html.

11. Aldo Palmisana, "Why Do Some Fish Normally Live in Freshwater and Others in Saltwater? How Can Some Fish Adapt to Both?" *Scientific American*, January 19, 1998, https://www.scientificamerican.com/article/why-do-some-fish-normally/.

12. "Swimmers Beware: The Most Dangerous Waters on Earth," The Rainforest Site, accessed June 8, 2023, https://blog.therainforestsite.greatergood.com/most-dangerous-waters/.

13. Jeff Bonaldi, "Crossing the Drake Passage? Everything You Need to Know," Explorers Passage, accessed May 11, 2023, https://explorerspassage.com/chronicles/the-drake-passage/.

14. Lindi Osborne, "What Tide Is Best for Your Favorite Water Activity?" The Swim Guide, February 12, 2020, https://www.theswimguide.org/2020/02/13/what-tide-is-best-for-your-favourite-water-activity/.

References

15. Ibid.

16. "The Douglas Sea State Scale," Jackson Parton, Solicitors, accessed June 8, 2023, https://jacksonparton.com/the-douglas-sea-state-scale.

17. Brown, *Rising Strong*. (Random House, 2017), ebook, page 136.

18. "(1857) Frederick Douglass, 'If There Is No Struggle, There Is No Progress,'" Black Past, accessed November 15, 2023, https://www.blackpast.org/african-american-history/1857-frederick-douglass-if-there-no-struggle-there-no- progress/.

19. "Frederick Douglass," Americans Who Tell the Truth, accessed November 15, 2023, https://americanswhotellthetruth.org/portraits/frederick-douglass/?gad_source=1&gclid=Cj0KCQiAr8eqBhD3ARIsAIe- buOpbt9PQ_Eszs8ihS3XyQZPfvT0FnrYv5dASaV4sCJ3Fx1hJm2ajw-MaAvjmEALw_wcB.

20. "The Lesser-Known Legacy of Frederick Douglass," Anti-Racism Commitment Coalition News, February 2023, https://joinarcc.org/arcc-news-the-lesser-known-legacy-of-frederick-douglass/.

21. Emma Martin, "Kalahari Acacia Woodlands," One Earth, accessed March 24, 2023, https://www.oneearth.org/ecoregions/kalahari-acacia-woodlands/.

22. Kristin Hissong, "Beachcomber's View: Science of Sea Glass," Coastal Review.org, June 12, 2019, https://coastalreview.org/2019/06/beachcombers-view-the-science-of-seaglass/.

23. Todd B. Bates, "Deep Roots in Plants Driven by Soil Hydrology," Rutgers University–New Brunswick, September 18, 2017, https://www.rutgers.edu/news/deep-roots-plants-driven-soil-hydrology.

24. Ralph Waldo Emerson, "Self-Reliance," *Essays, First Series*, (1841), https://archive.vcu.edu/english/engweb/transcendentalism/authors/emerson/essays.

25. Tony Evans, *Detours* (B&H Books, 2017), ebook, week 4, day 1.

26. Brown, *Daring Greatly* (Random House, 2012), ebook, page 69.

27. Linda Jereb, *Genuine Sea Glass*, By the Sea Jewelry, accessed March 24, 2023, https://bytheseajewelry.com/genuine-sea-glass-how-to-tell-the-difference-between-real-fake/.

28. Ibid.

29. Jeremy Hall, "How to Find Sea Glass (10 Tips for Collecting Sea Glass), Rock Seeker, last updated July 30, 2024, 20:12, https://rockseeker.com/how-to-find-sea-glass/.

30. Investopedia Team, "Intrinsic Value Defined and How It's Determined in Investing and Business," Investopedia, last updated June 5, 2024, https://www.investopedia.com/terms/i/intrinsicvalue.asp.

31. Ibid.

32. April Knecht, "All About Grade Sea Glass Rarity and Quality," Real Sea Glass, accessed October 12, 2022, https://realseaglass.com/pages/all-about-grading-sea-glass-rarity-quality.

About the Author

Jamie Lee Zenteno

Coming from a twenty-year background in ministry and community leadership, Jamie Lee Zenteno is well-seasoned in delivering the gospel. Through experiences that God has allowed in her life, she believes that the Lord has given her the ability to see people as He does. Jamie Zenteno Ministries was forged in 2023 with hope of serving others in their healing journeys.

Jamie Zenteno was born to wonderful parents and raised in the small town of Santa Fe, Texas. She continues to reside in her hometown with her two wonderful daughters. Often, you may find them spending weekends at a softball field or horse arena.

www.ingramcontent.com/pod-product-compliance
Lightning Source LLC
Chambersburg PA
CBHW070538090426
42735CB00013B/3012